Royal Scots
of the LMS

E. S. COX   W. A. TUPLIN
JOHN POWELL   P. G. JOHNSON

Edited by DOUGLAS DOHERTY

LONDON
IAN ALLAN

First Published 1970

SBN 7110 0165 0

Published by Ian Allan Ltd, Shepperton, Surrey, and printed in the United Kingdom by the Press at Coombelands, Addlestone, Weybridge, Surrey

Contents

Introduction

THIS IS a portrait of a famous class of steam locomotives, the LMS Royal Scots. The portrait is a composite painting with brushwork by a number of artists.

My enjoyable task has been mainly to organise the execution of the work, from a mind's eye vision to the completed work as here presented. After erecting the easel and canvas facing the required scene and sketching in the outlines, I placed the brushes in the hands of other artists to add life and lustre to my outlines.

These other artists really selected themselves, being proven masters in their fields. The colours are drawn from their varied experiences with these fine locomotives. Let me introduce them.

Mr E. S. Cox was of course, a former Assistant Chief Mechanical Engineer of British Railways, and was responsible for the design of the fleet of Standard passenger and freight locomotives and rolling stock. Since retirement from BR in 1965, Mr Cox has enriched the realms of steam locomotive literature with his books for Ian Allan Ltd.

John Powell may not be so widely known to enthusiasts, though as 45671, Mr Powell penned a superb series of articles for *Trains Illustrated* at intervals from November 1957. Steeped in LMS practice from his days as a Derby apprentice. Forsaking motive power, Mr Powell held various appointments including Projects Officer responsible for the introduction of Freightliner and merry-go-round coal operations in Scotland. After a while as Traffic Officer for the Scottish Region of Freightliners Ltd, Mr Powell moved to his present post as Planning Officer (Operations) for the Channel Tunnel Organisation of British Railways Board.

Driver Johnson commenced his railway career in the time honoured tradition as a locomotive cleaner, at Wellington (Shropshire) GWR in 1944. Transferred to Gresty Lane, Crewe, and then to Crewe North shed, Driver Johnson progressed through the links before moving to the South shed, reaching Registered Driver in 1961. He still pounds up and down the West Coast main line, though less gloriously than of yesteryear, now at the controls of diesel and electric locomotives.

No one is better fitted to offer a critical appreciation of the Royal Scots than Dr W. A. Tuplin, Professor of Applied Mechanics at

7

Sheffield University. He began unofficial observation of steam locomotives at the age of three and right to the end of steam on British Railways continued to find unofficial ways of working them. A forthright and independent thinker and respected engineer.

My own connection with steam matters is purely as a "mad railway photographer". I have yet to recover from the blow of steam's disappearance, so inextricably was my life bound up with it. Life goes on of course, but I find small regular doses of reminiscence a welcome diversion from my "with it" job as a Training Officer with an industrial training board.

For relevant dabs on the canvas I would like to thank camera artists F. R. Hebron, George Barlow, W. Potter, T. G. Hepburn, M. W. Earley and L. Hanson. Acknowledgement is also due to the Public Relations Officer of British Rail's London Midland Region for the excellent selection of official photographs he kindly made available to me.

At the time of writing, I am informed by David Jenkinson that the switch between No 6100 and No 6152 for the 1933 American tour has not yet been verified by the existance of official records. In any case as Mr Cox points out, the engine that did go was considerably different from either 6100 or 6152 in their original condition—new bogie, new axleboxes, new springing and almost certainly a replacement boiler.

DOUGLAS DOHERTY

SHEFFIELD
February 1970

Mechanical Development

by E. S. COX, FIMechE

THE ROYAL SCOT class of locomotives of the LMS Railway were in many ways the most remarkable series of express passenger engines to have served the railways of this country. Reaching a total of only 71 engines they remained rostered to important main line duties from their first unusual and dramatic inception in 1927 through a complete modernisation and rebuilding in 1943 until the last one was withdrawn in the late 1960s. It can also be claimed on their behalf that they were the most successful and efficient 4-6-0 engines to have run on any British railway.

Forty-seven years ago the London Midland & Scottish Railway came into being, and the locomotives it inherited from its constituent companies proved ill-suited to provide the improved services which the new company wished to offer, in particular on the West Coast Main Line between Euston and Glasgow. George Hughes, the first CME, had outlined simple expansion Pacifics, and his successor, Sir Henry Fowler, was in 1926 actively engaged in designing a Compound version of the same wheel arrangement. On the other hand the independent Operating and Motive Power Departments in the persons of Follows and Anderson wished to perpetuate the small engine policy of the former Midland Railway. In the face of such divided counsel in its principal officers, the Management obtained in that year loan of a GW Castle class engine, which during a month's trial between Euston and Carlisle indicated unambiguously the kind of head end power which was necessary.

The LMS Company's latest West Coast service had to be handled by two Midland compounds between Glasgow and Carnforth, and by a Claughton piloted by a George V south to the metropolis so that the need for a new engine capable of giving improved running single handed became urgent and imperative, and thus was born the Royal Scot locomotive.

Quick managerial decisions were made to abandon Fowler's compound Pacific ideas, and to concentrate upon a 4-6-0 which would include the essentials which had been so triumphantly indicated by the visitor from Swindon—a large boiler carrying a high working pressure, long-travel valve gear and man-sized axleboxes. With the important features thus accepted, no need was felt to copy the

9

visitor too slavishly, three cylinders were decided upon instead of four, and a high degree superheater was incorporated.

Since early delivery was imperative, the work of making the working drawings and of building the 50 locomotives which were required was given to the North British Locomotive Company of Glasgow. With a vast drawing office and two building works available, this company performed the astonishing feat of having all 50 engines delivered within 12 months of the placing of the order. The initial diagram was prepared at Derby, and failing any response from Swindon to a request for detail drawings of the Castle, a full set of drawings of the contemporary Lord Nelson 4-cylinder 4-6-0 engine were obtained from the Southern Railway. Although available for overall guidance, very little use was made of these drawings, except in respect of the firebox. The basic design followed established Derby practice in all details and in particular, the cylinders and long travel valve gear were modelled from those of the 2300 class 2-6-4 tank which was being designed simultaneously in the Derby drawing office.

His compound proposals having been abruptly rejected, Sir Henry Fowler was naturally not too interested at first in their successor and the work of doing the actual design fell upon Herbert Chambers, the Derby Chief Draughtsman, and his principal assistants, with, of course, much valuable help from their counterparts at Springburn.

The new engine thus started under every seeming disadvantage, a hurried initial decision, 50 engines to be built straight off the board, a very short delivery time, a CME only lukewarm towards the new project, and the design itself being undertaken committee-wise by LMS and NB Loco staff in collaboration. But this time the Jeremiahs who feared the worst were triumphantly routed for the machine which emerged in August and commenced its full scale trials in October 1927 was a magnificent production which, from the very first, delivered performance and economy such as had never previously been experienced on the LMS and its constituents, and which surpassed even what *Launceston Castle* itself had achieved the year before.

There were three 18in × 26in cylinders, each with its independent Walschaert valve gear, driving coupled wheels 6ft 9in dia giving, with a working pressure of 250 lb/sq in, a starting tractive effort of 33,150 lb. Valve travel as built was 6.3in maximum with $1\frac{1}{2}$in steam lap and nil exhaust clearance; lead was $\frac{3}{16}$in. This parallel boiler had a maximum outside diameter of 5ft 9in, and had 27 large $5\frac{1}{8}$in dia and 180 small 2in tubes, 14ft 6in between tubeplates. Heating surfaces were: tubes 1892sq ft; firebox 189sq ft; superheater 416sq ft; grate area

31.2sq ft. The boiler was pitched 9ft 3½in above rail level which gave ample room under the grate for a disposition of ashpan over the trailing coupled axle which permitted free entry of air for combustion even towards the end of six hours' running. The Derby authorities had had trouble with earlier attempts to fit "drumhead" front tubeplates, although these had become commonplace in more recent British practice. Accordingly the Scot was provided with the older arrangement of tubeplate secured to the barrel by an angle ring, which feature required a smokebox large in diameter in relation to the boiler barrel—in this case its outside dimension was 6ft 7⅛in. This was the reason for the exceptionally short chimney, only 7 7/16 in high which this engine carried within an overall height of 13ft 2½in. The Derby practice of using a parallel rather than a taper chimney was followed, and the 1ft 3in diameter chosen for the Scot was not, as has so often been done on other classes, given a bolder profile by incorporating an outer casing of larger diameter in the chimney construction. Being not only short but narrow, the rather insignificant chimney quite spoiled the front end appearance of these otherwise handsome engines. On the other hand, although selected according to the empirical methods of the time, the chimney proportions were closely akin to those ultimately developed by Ell as a result of his later work on the Swindon stationary plant, and this fortunate circumstance provided a draughting arrangement admirably suited to 3-cylinder propulsion, so that an excellent steaming quality was the result.

Maximum axle weight was 20 tons 18cwts but the effect of this upon the track was mitigated by a hammer blow of only 0.3 tons per axle at 87mph—0.9 tons for the whole engine. The standard Midland 3500 gallon tender carrying 7 tons of coal was fitted at first; the total weight of the engine in working order was 84 tons 18cwt, and with tender the weight was 129 tons 2cwt.

In tune with the publicity attending the putting to work of these engines, they became the first LMS new construction to bear names. Half of them were named after famous regiments of the British Army, and half bore the names of early locomotives at the dawn of railway history. A pleasing feature in connection with the latter was the provision of a small brass plate below the name proper, having engraved upon it the lineaments of the particular old engine whose name was being used. The running numbers were 6100–6149.

Twenty further engines of identical design were built in the railway workshops at Derby in 1929, numbers 6150–6169. The last engine of the series, No 6399, was again built by the North British Locomotive

Company, the normal boiler being in this case replaced by an ultra high pressure boiler of German design and origin sponsored in this country by the Superheater Company. The arrangement was most complex, there being three inter-woven portions generating steam at 1400, 900 and 250 lb/sq in respectively. The first of these steam pressures worked in a closed circuit whose purpose was to generate steam at 900 lb/sq in in a large drum above the firebox, this steam being fed direct to a single inside HP cylinder $11\frac{1}{2}$in dia $\times$ 26in stroke. Exhaust from this cylinder was mixed with steam at 250 lb/sq in produced from a normal type of barrel in the forward part of the boiler, and was fed to two 18in $\times$ 26in LP cylinders outside the frames. The nominal tractive effort remained the same, but the weight of the engine was increased by $2\frac{1}{4}$ tons. The object of the exercise was to raise the thermal efficiency. (Drawing on page 58.)

The new engines were put to work at once on the heaviest and fastest duties on the Western and Scottish Divisions. The star turn was the Royal Scot service which in summer ran the 299 miles from Euston to Carlisle non-stop at an average of 52mph with 420 tons train load. This was regularly done at first on only 5.4 tons of coal, 40.4lb per mile, giving a consumption per drawbar horsepower hour of 3.58lb. Other duties involved through running with a stop at Crewe, taking 500 tons south thereof, and the engines also took up duty with the most important trains on the Liverpool, Holyhead and Manchester services. Only No 6399 proved obstinate, and various troubles, of which difficulties with water circulation and with the high pressure feed pumps were the principal, prevented this engine from entering revenue-earning service.

The Royal Scots remained to outward view in their original condition for some fifteen years, except only for the later fitting of smoke deflector plates and substitution of the original 3500 gallon tenders by larger high-sided versions carrying 4000 gallons of water and nine tons of coal. Internally however, the intensive heavy work to which they were subject revealed some weaknesses which called for modification in design. Earliest of these was an alarming increase in coal consumption, and the story has often been told of how, within two years of building, nine tons of coal were in some cases needed to reach Carlisle, in place of the five or just over which had sufficed at first. This was due to the single wide ring, with which each piston-valve head was fitted, not remaining steam tight, so that an undesirable proportion of the steam supplied by the boiler passed straight up the chimney without doing useful work in the cylinders. The cure was found by substituting multiple narrow rings on each piston head, four at first, and eventually six. The last 14 of the second 1930 batch of Scots were so fitted and one of them, No 6158, with six rings per head and subject also to some minor changes in valve events, not only reduced steam wastage due to internal leakage from 80 per cent to 8 per cent over the period of piston and valve examination, but also gave a satisfying improvement in efficiency in new condition, reducing the coal consumption per DBHP hour from 3.58lb to 3.17lb on the Euston–Carlisle run with the same loads, timings and coal as for No 6100 as originally built.

All of the Scots were eventually altered to the pattern of 6158, and it was not only on heavy trains that a satisfying economy now became the norm. When, as was inevitable from time to time, light loads had to be handled, it is on record that with train weights such as 214 tons from Carlisle to Crewe and 268 tons on to Euston, only $3\frac{3}{4}$ tons of coal were burned over the whole 299 miles, giving a consumption of $27\frac{1}{2}$lb per mile, a figure quite unattainable by any of the smaller engines more usually rostered to loads of this kind.

The second trouble concerned coupled axle boxes. Although of generous size, their design followed the Midland practice of employing manganese bronze castings for the body of the box. As this material was not a bearing metal, brass strips were dovetailed into the box which, when bridged by white metal, formed a composite bearing surface which rode upon the axle journal. This assembly was thought to give best heat dissipation but it could not withstand the heavy side thrusts of such a big engine travelling fast. Bad riding due to excessive lateral wear came first and then as the boxes lost the firmness of new construction, and repair procedure was unable to regain it, hot bearings began to mount up. These, which totalled only 25 for the 70 active engines in 1930, became 75 in 1931 and 102 in 1932. The axlebox was certainly an item which the designers would have done better to copy from *Launceston Castle* in 1926, and with the advent of Stanier as CME of the LMS in 1932, the Swindon type of axlebox consisting of a steel casting with pressed-in brass became adopted for all new construction and was in due time applied to the Royal Scot class. The first engine was altered thus in 1933, and with 36 engines altered by the end of that year, heating cases fell to 43. Eventually hot boxes were for all practical purposes eliminated by this change of design.

In passing, reference may be made, in contra-distinction to the case of the axleboxes, to the fact that of all 3-cylinder engines of which there is record the Scots were the most trouble-free as regards their middle big ends. Gresley's anxieties on the LNER are well known, and Stanier's 5X class came into its share of troubles to the extent that many of these engines were fitted with tell-tale stink bombs to give warning to the driver when disaster was impending. But the Scots throughout their lives caused little anxiety in this respect.

The third weakness in these otherwise excellent machines was a hidden one. British designers in those far-off days thought a bogie was a bogie, and saw no reason why the value of the spring side control which they provided on a big 4–6–0, ought to be any more than on a small 4–4–0. The Scots were thus built with only ¾ ton of initial side control, the same as on the Midland compounds. Nobody realised that the lively riding of the Scots, contained an element of danger in that when so massive a machine began to sway laterally about a vertical line through its centre of gravity, but was insufficiently controlled from the front end, there could, when engine and track elasticities came into resonance, arise a tendency for lateral oscillation to build up towards the possibility of derailment. Such an eventuality did in fact occur in January 1930 at Weaver Junction on the West Coast main line when one of these engines was traversing a high speed turn out at a permitted 70mph and a most unpleasant accident took place. Even the assistance of so famous a scientist as Professor W. E. Dalby, failed to locate the cause at that time, and it was the purest chance, quite unconnected with the findings on the mishap, which in 1931 led Derby to put up the value of the bogie side control to two tons as a safeguard against a plague of broken springs. This happened to be just sufficient to tip the scales, and the engines ran safely in their original condition thereafter. But it is possible to shudder at what might have been the possibilities had the engines continued unaltered in this respect.

Of miscellaneous events with the original engines, may be mentioned the alteration of No 6116 in 1931 to work at 200 lb/sq in. This was not due to any particular trouble or high boiler maintenance, but arose from the observation that drivers rarely if ever worked the engines with full regulator, and the consideration that if only 200lb and under was reaching the steam chests, then provision of a higher boiler pressure seemed rather to be wasted. On Dynameter Car trials, No 6116 showed no measurable difference in timekeeping, steaming or coal and water consumption, only now the men found they needed to work full regulator to carry out their rosters.

Since the boiler was designed to withstand 250lb/sq in and gave rise to satisfactorily low maintenance costs, there seemed no practical point in altering any further engines in this way. High pressure up to about 300lb/sq in does not of itself cause higher maintenance costs per mile run in the Stephenson boiler. Integrity of design and quality of water are the determining factors in this cost.

In their later years, the 25 engines which carried the names and effigies of historic early locomotives, had them gradually taken off and replaced by the names of further regiments in the Army. It can be held that to name a locomotive, a single entity, after a regiment comprising numerous men, is nonsense, but since each such naming ceremony could be undertaken in an aura of publicity this was held to be a valid enough reason for suppressing the much more pleasing earlier names.

William Stanier's name has been mentioned above in connection with axleboxes, and his appointment at the beginning of 1932 as Chief Mechanical Engineer of the LMS brought many changes to the locomotive practice of that railway which have been amply recorded elsewhere. It was inevitable therefore, that he brought changes to the Royal Scot class which at the time of his advent was still the premier express engine class in his new domain. The engines were in those days apparently working at the peak of their form, and except in the matter of the axleboxes, no further alterations seemed to be necessary. Nevertheless important modifications were in fact initiated over the next 10 years which it is now proposed to describe.

Very soon after Stanier's arrival an invitation was received to send a locomotive and train to the USA to be exhibited at the forthcoming "Century of Progress" exhibition at Chicago. Although design work had commenced upon the Pacific class, eventually known as the Princess Royal, it could not possibly be built in time, so the decision was made to send an engine of the Royal Scot class. A suitable unit due for shopping was selected, but if he could not send an engine of his own design Stanier was determined to make his mark upon the one which did go overseas. To this end the "Scot" was completely reshod, being fitted with new coupled axleboxes based upon Swindon design as had been decided upon for the class as a whole, and in addition a new bogie and new springing were provided. The bogie had widely spaced side bearers taking the weight of the superstructure, and an arrangement of compensated side control springs gave improved lateral stability by cutting out all lost motion.

This design had first appeared in this country on the three French De Glehn compounds purchased by the Great Western Railway at the turn of the century, and had been applied by Churchward and his successors to Swindon bogies. Stanier thought so highly of its properties that he used it on all his new designs for the LMS, but only this single Royal Scot engine was fitted before the general rebuilding which began in 1943. The same comments, except that they did not originate from France, apply to the new springs and spring rigging with which Stanier sought to improve the riding and the life of the springs between repairs. The engine, which bore the number 6100 and the name *Royal Scot*, made its appearance at the Chicago Exhibition in 1933 and afterwards travelled under steam with its train over 11,194 miles on various American railroads, in the course of all of which it was seen by over three million people. As in the case of the visit of the GWR engine *King George V* in 1927, the fine workmanship and relatively silent operation of the Scot made a big impression upon a public accustomed to a more robust head-end operation of their trains. Upon its return, 6100's nameplate was suitably enlarged to retail some account of its exploits.

Stanier's next operation upon the Royal Scot class arose from the final failure of No 6399, the engine with the Schmidt-Henschel high pressure boiler, to become capable of revenue earning work. Soon after completion this engine had killed one man and badly injured another, due to bursting of one of the tubes forming the firebox lining. This was due to uncertain natural circulation of the water through these tubes, a weakness which proved impossible to correct. As already mentioned, there were other troubles as well, and after languishing inactive in the Derby paint shop over a number of years, Stanier had the engine steamed in his presence as final confirmation of its worthlessness before recommending its complete rebuilding into a normal kind of locomotive. Re-numbered 6170, the resurrection which appeared in 1935, was an enlarged version of the same designer's 5X class 3-cylinder 4-6-0s which were currently being built in large numbers, A taper boiler was provided, with new inside cylinders and new smokebox, and all of the detail features and fittings which made up the Stanier *marque*.

Cylinder dimensions, grate area and working pressure remained the same as on the original Scot, but the firebox heating surface was increased to 195sq ft and the tube surface slightly reduced to 1669sq ft. A 28 element superheater gave 360sq ft of surface. The total weight of the engine in working order was 17cwt less. Although capable of good work, this engine was at first something of a disappointment because of its uncertain steaming qualities. It will be remembered that Stanier's earlier 5X class engines suffered from the same weakness which was due to too free a passage for the hot gases through the tubes, which produced high smokebox temperatures at the cost of inadequate heat transfer to the water. On Dynamometer

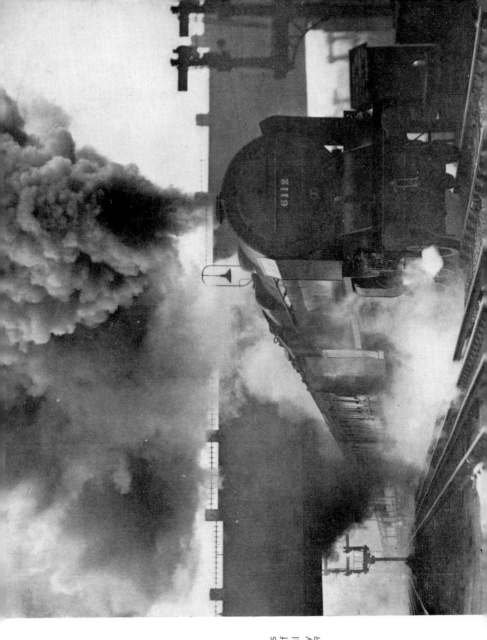

No 6112 climbs Camden bank out of Euston with the "Royal Scot" in the early 1930s *IBR*

B

No 6110 *Royal Scot* in works grey paint as built, without smoke deflectors and with small tender   [BR

No 6147 *Courier* soon after entry into service, with LMS crest on cabside and number on tender

No 6149 *Lady of The Lake*, the last of the NBL Co-built members of the class, at Crewe North. Nos 6125 to 6149 originally received names of old time locomotives; they also carried an etched in brass outline of the original locomotive on a plate beneath the nameplate. All the names and plates were later removed and replaced with regimental names   [T. G. Hepburn

Above: No 6110 *Grenadier Guardsman* heads the down "Midday Scot", formed of ex-LNW 12–wheel "Corridor" stock, past Kenton in April 1928 *[M. W. Earley]*

Below: No 6100 *Royal Scot* at the head of a London-Liverpool express soon after entry into service

On Friday, April 27, 1928, the LMS stole a march on the LNER, which was to inaugurate non-stop running between Kings Cross and Edinburgh the following Monday, by running the "Royal Scot" in two parts from Euston non-stop to Glasgow and Edinburgh. The Glasgow portion was hauled by "Royal Scot" No 6113 *Cameronian,* the Edinburgh section by compound 4-4-0 No 1054. According to contemporary accounts these arduous runs were achieved by volunteer crews, whose only stipulation was that adequate tenders should be provided. This picture, taken at the time, shows No 6113 fitted with the tender it used for the non-stop run, on an up Western Division express at Kenton

No 6132 *Phoenix* passing Oxenholme with the down "Midday Scot". Note Caledonian Railway route indicator on smokebox. Next to the engine is a GWR coach from Plymouth   [F. R. Hebron

Train engine No 6109 *Royal Engineer* has just taken on as pilot LNWR "Precursor" class 4-4-0 No 5263 *Oceanic* restarting the down "Royal Scot" from Oxenholme around 1930 *[F.R. Hebron*

Newly built and waiting at Derby to take on a London-bound express is No 6145, soon to be named *Condor*   [*T. G. Hepburn*

The 10.30am Euston-Liverpool leaves Euston around 1930 behind No 6147 *Courier*   [*BR*

Running with temporary indicating shelter for testing purposes is No 6158 *The Loyal Regiment*
[F. R. Hebron

No 6122 *Royal Ulster Rifleman* heads the down "Royal Scot" on Bushey troughs around 1930
[F. R. Hebron

Above: Another view at Wavertree—No 6144 *Honourable Artillery Company* heads a Euston express   [*Eric Treacy*

Left: After fitting with smoke deflectors—a striking shot of No 6143 *The South Staffordshire Regiment* storming out of Liverpool for London   [*Eric Treacy*

Above left: Smoke deflection experiments before the adoption of full side-shields—No 6141 *Caledonian* with small "shovel" behind the chimney

Above: Another type of chimney deflector on No 6133 *Vulcan*
[F. R. Hebron

Below left: No 6100 *Royal Scot* for a time carried a larger version of the "shovel" rim. The train is an up Perth express leaving Carlisle   [F. R. Hebron

Below: Yet another experiment to lift exhaust steam and smoke clear of the boiler, and improve driver visibility No 6161 *King's Own* at Crewe. Note also the built-up tender to increase coal-carrying capacity   [T. G. Hepburn

In 1933, the "Royal Scot" locomotive and train toured the USA and Canada. No 6152 was the loco that made the trip, after exchanging names and numbers with the original No 6100 (the original identities were never re-assumed). The new 6100 is shown ready for shipment, complete with electric headlamp and smokebox door nameplate   [BR

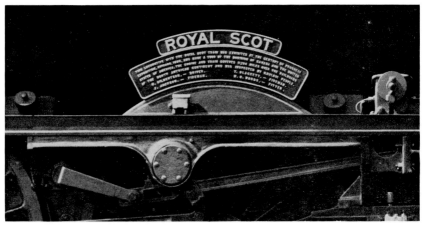

One of the plaques affixed to No 6100's splashers after the US tour. When No 6100 was rebuilt under the Stanier regime, the plaques were modified with the addition of "Prior to conversion" above the top line of the inscription   [W. Potter

No 6100 on show during the US tour

The smoke and steam lifting experiments finally led to the adoption of full deflectors of the type shown here on No 6130 *The West Yorkshire Regiment*

Next change was the fitting of bigger, high-sided tenders, as here attached to No 6160 *Queen Victoria's Rifleman*

The final LMS livery—No 6145 *The Duke of Wellington's Regiment (West Riding)*

Above: The Royal Scots were capable of heavy haulage and rarely needed piloting. When the motive power department did resort to double heading, it was usually with a smaller locomotive, either Midland Class 2 4-4-0 or a Jubilee 4-6-0. The sight of two Royal Scots on the same train however was decidedly rare, but Nos 6167 and 6165 worked the down "Lancastrian" from Euston to Manchester on May 1, 1937; the pair are seen here approaching Bushey   *[E. R. Wethersett*

Below: Up Anglo-Scottish Express at Euxton, Lancs—note smokebox decoration of No 6136 *The Border Regiment*
[Eric Treacy

Above right: In BR ownership—unrebuilt No 46141 *The North Staffordshire Regiment* climbs out of Euston
[Eric Treacy

Below right: One of the last to survive unrebuilt, No 46137 *The Prince of Wales Volunteers, South Lancashire* heads a Liverpool-Newcastle express through Manchester Victoria in June, 1952
[B Yale

The experimental compound locomotive No 6399 *Fury*, built by NBL Co   [BR

Eventually the chassis of *Fury* was fitted with a new boiler and three simple cylinders. As such it was renumbered 6170 and renamed *British Legion*. The raked back steam pipes were eventually modified   [BR

The final look of No 46170 *British Legion* ex-*Fury*   [P. Ransome-Wallis

Car test, a smokebox full of char almost up to the top of the blastpipe after a run of 200 miles, showed all too clearly where the trouble lay, accompanied as it was bound to be, by a relatively high coal consumption. As built, No 6170's boiler had small tubes 2⅛in dia 14ft 3in long in conjunction with 5⅛in diameter flue tubes housing superheater elements 1⅛in diameter. When re-tubed with more small tubes 1⅞in diameter fitted with superheater elements 1¼in diameter and when equipped with a double blast pipe and chimney to combine adequate gas velocity with improved evaporative capacity of the tubes, the engine in its later days became a much improved performer. This tuning up did as much for No 6170 as it did for the errant 5X engines and brought both up to the point of meeting the full requirements of the Operating Department.

The last phase in the life of the Royal Scot class was its complete rebuilding from 1943 onwards. No 6170 has often been described as the prototype for this massive conversion, but it is only true in the most general way, and indeed the possession of a taper-shaped boiler and continuation of use of 3-cylinders are about the only common factors. In order to trace the influences which led to this final alteration, it is necessary to turn aside for a moment to the history of the smaller 5X class already referred to. By 1935 these latter were in real trouble, not only because of defective boiler proportions as already pointed out, but due also to unreliability of the inside big ends. Amongst various schemes for their improvement, one prepared at Derby was for a trial conversion substituting two outside cylinders only for the existing three, and for the fitting of a larger taper boiler. The 2-cylinder proposal was not pursued, but the boiler, differing from that of No 6170 in having a barrel 1ft 3in shorter, and employing 198 small tubes 1¾in diameter in place of 180 of 1⅞in diameter was the true prototype of that eventually provided for the rebuilt Scots. This was the boiler used when, during the war, Coleman, chief designer at Derby, was given his head by Stanier to do a larger and more powerful version of the 5X, eliminating once and for all its defects. Nos 5735/6 of this class were thus rebuilt in 1943 and it was these engines rather than No 6170 which were the true model for what followed. Besides the boiler, important changes were made in cylinder design. The work of Chapelon in France had before the war opened the eyes of designers to the advantage of improving steam flow by the provision of ports and passages of increased sectional area, and Coleman took full advantage of such possibilities in his design of the cylinders for No 5735 with a view to obtaining a clear-cut improvement in relative power output. In addition, certain changes in

c

valve events were introduced, more lead and less lap and the provision of some exhaust clearance, which favoured lively performance rather than the utmost economy. As a further insurance against derailment the value of the initial bogie side control was at the same time increased to four tons. The result was that the converted engines not only far surpassed the 5Xs, but they proved themselves superior to the Scots, and the drivers and inspectors acclaimed with much joy this greatly improved traffic tool.

When the application of all this to the Royal Scot class, an obvious follow on, came to be considered, Fairburn had succeeded Stanier in the CME's Office. The change was by no means a foregone conclusion, for the rebuilding was an expensive one and the still continuing war put a brake on new projects. Since a number of Scot boilers would shortly be falling due for renewal, most careful consideration was given to the more economical course of building replacement boilers to the old design and merely improving the axle boxes. What swayed the outcome, other than strongly expressed pressure from the users, was the fact that the smokebox and its connection to the cylinders on the old Scots was becoming thoroughly worn out and difficult to keep air-tight. So the decision was taken to convert the whole class in batches as boilers fell in, exactly to the pattern of 5735, except only that the original cab sides were retained, having a single side window and cut away portion at the rear.

The Railway Press has recorded many fine runs with these engines as thus finally rebuilt, and in the Interchange Trials of 1948 when they were pitted on equal terms against the most modern designs, they gave so good an account of themselves that C. J. Allen was able to write:

> [1] "Relative to the moderate dimensions and weight and the simplicity of design of these 4–6–0s . . . I should be inclined to rate their best performance above anything else I witnessed during the test weeks . . . moreover the drawbar HP outputs of 1750 to 1800 exerted by the Scots on some of the climbs must surely constitute a record for any British 4–6–0 design of no more than 83 tons in weight."

That such performance was not bought too dearly, allowing for valve events which as mentioned above favoured high power, was indicated by an overall coal consumption of 3.38lb per DBHP hour covering the whole of the runs which were made during the tests.

After all the thought and work which had been lavished through

[1] *The Locomotive Exchange* by Cecil J. Allen (Ian Allan, 1949)

the years, it could have been expected that the Royal Scot would finally become as perfect as any steam locomotive could be in this fallible world. While, however, its record showed it to be among the very best, one defect remained with it to the end, namely rough riding. When, after the war, interest in locomotive development was resumed and staff could be found for further investigation, an intensive onslaught was mounted against this trouble. There were several ingredients. The high value of the bogie side control which had been introduced as an insurance against such derailments as that at Weaver Junction tended to "fix" the front end of the engine and concentrate all the bucking and rolling at the back end. Some reduction in bogie side control values helped, as did careful rebalancing of all the coupled wheels. Stiffer springs were fitted while development of excessive lateral wear on axleboxes and horns was limited by the fitting of manganese liners. All of these measures helped, but they did not eliminate the characteristic back end movement, which is probably inherent in a large relatively short 4-6-0 with a high centre of gravity. Nothing dangerous remained, but still grounds for complaint when a run down engine encountered less than perfect track. It was at this end of the spectrum that a Pacific gave better opportunity for the assurance of controlled good riding.

In their 40 years of main line service, including much running on the Midland Division in later years, the 71 engines must have accumulated something like 180 million miles, and it would be interesting to know what they earned in total for their owners. Sufficient has been said, however, to indicate that they were a very good investment, that they gave better rather than inferior service as they got older, and that they enshrined all that was best in British locomotive tradition, even although many hands and minds, rather than a single overpowering personality had been responsible for their development.

A Critical Appreciation

by W. A. TUPLIN, DSc, FIMechE

THE "GROUPING" of the railways of Britain at the beginning of 1923 was bound to create difficulties in all departments. Where the aim was to fuse railways of comparable size and status into a new whole, competition between individuals for the best jobs and competition between different schools of thought on technical matters were sure to breed antagonism and to retard the accomplishment of anything like harmony.

The Great Western group was the best of all in this respect simply because the Great Western Railway was by far the biggest member of the group and so there could hardly be any internal competition.

Conditions were worst in the London, Midland & Scottish Group because there the two major members, the London & North Western Railway and the Midland Railway, were of about the same size and of about the same general technical excellence. Midland management dominated the LMS for non-technical reasons but it did not make any immediate impression on locomotive design largely because the Midland locomotive "chief", Sir Henry Fowler, was a manager and a workshop organiser with no special interest in locomotive design. He had consequently to rely on the opinions of his technical assistants to a greater extent than most Chief Mechanical Engineers found necessary and as there were sharply contrasted schools of thought at Crewe, Derby and Horwich he did not know what to do. The best he could think of when it became clear that more locomotive power was required for the main-line services of the LMS was to build more 4-4-0s of the Midland Compound design dating back some twenty years. Midland policy had long been to avoid working engines hard. Express passenger train loads were very severely limited; when a need arose to overstep the formal limit by even two per cent, an extra engine was provided. On the North Western, on the other hand, main line expresses were about twice as heavy as the maxima the Midland allowed for engines of similar size and if a couple of extra coaches were added to a train, no extra engine was provided; they simply thrashed the regular engine a bit more than usual.

So North Western engines continued to run the West Coast main-line trains and the operating department grumbled about the way the engines had to be overworked. The Midland drawing office at

Derby produced detailed designs of a 4-cylinder compound Pacific and the works were ready to get going, but the operating department objected that their turn-tables were not long enough for engines as big as that and ex-North Western officials were up in arms against any sort of "compound". They had had their fill of Webb compounds before 1900 and the Midland compounds that they had had after 1923 had made no better impression on them.

The Lancashire & Yorkshire had, in 1921, rebuilt 4-cylinder 4–6–0s with great advantage and there was disappointment at Horwich when these were found to be inferior to the Crewe Claughtons on West Coast work.

The Caledonian people were firmly convinced that only Caledonian engines could possibly be any good for Scottish trains.

LMS motive power was in a mess and as it showed no sign of sorting itself out, the directors looked around. They noticed the Great Western triumphing over the LNER in the 1925 locomotive exchange, they tried a Great Western Castle on the West Coast main-line and found it to be better than any LMS engine had ever been, and they noticed ex-Great Western engineers developing on the Southern Railway the Lord Nelson 4–6–0 that was virtually a "super-Castle". So, disregarding Sir Henry Fowler, they arranged for a couple of LMS locomotive engineers to get information from the Southern about the Lord Nelson and to use it as a basis for the design of something as good or better to run the LMS West Coast trains. Moreover, the main "day" trains, up and down, were to be glamourised with new stock and the title "Royal Scot" for the summer services starting in July 1927 and the new engines were wanted for then. As the decision was made as late as November 1926 this was quite impossible, but of course directors tend to be a bit like that. In actual fact a most valiant effort was made to meet this absurd requirement and the first of the new engines was running, although not run-in, during August 1927. Moreover the brash step had been taken of ordering 50 locomotives of the untried design, and this "came off"; the only difficulty with the new engines was that they were inclined to start away on their own if left with cylinder-cocks closed and brakes not fully applied.

All this meant quick work in design, crisp organisation and quick work by the North British Locomotive Company who built the 50 engines. The collaboration between LMS and SR designers was not publicly admitted until many years had elapsed but the close similarity of the designs was noticed in 1928 (*Railway Magazine*, March 1928, p241) by someone who had not had the least hint of any such collaboration, simply from examination of sectional drawings published by *The Engineer*.

There was obvious similarity in the downward slope from front to back of the roof of the outer firebox, the shape of the windowed side sheets of the cab, the shape of the regulator-handle, the type of fire-door, the use of a soot-blower, and the horizontal position of the whistle. All these features were new to the LMS.

There was very close correspondence between the two designs in main dimensions of the boiler and the tubes. Each firebox had a partly sloped grate, but that of the Scot was somewhat deeper and had noticeably greater height of the brick arch above the grate. This difference may have had greater significance than appeared at the time. The Scots turned out to be very much more satisfactory engines than were the Nelsons which could never be relied upon to beat the Southern King Arthur 4-6-0s. In the writer's view this was due to the greater difficulty of firing the (flat/slightly-sloped) grate of the Nelson. On the LMS, however, the men were used to Claughton fireboxes and found no special difficulty in firing Scots.

It was remarkable that the Lord Nelson had been given the old-fashioned wrapper-type smokebox when on the adjacent Great Western Railway (to look no further) the superior cylindrical smokebox had been a standard feature for a quarter of a century. The LMS should certainly have adopted it in the new design but—and this is a practical point—the shortage of available time discouraged the designer from any unnecessary departure from established LMS practice. Even so, the very marked difference in diameter between the smokebox and the boiler lagging plates seems to lack technical justification; the very fat smokebox and the correspondingly tiny chimney did however tend to conceal from immediate notice any resemblance between the new engine and any predecessor. The difference in external appearance between the LMS engine and its Southern progenitor was indeed remarkable in view of their similarity in main dimensions.

The worst feature of the Royal Scots (as these engines were called when they took over the train of that name in September 1927) and an unnecessary one, was the hiding of the rear end of the inside cylinder block and much of its valve gear as far out of reach as possible under the smokebox and over the bogie. If the Lord Nelson wheelbase had been adopted, the cylinder could have been placed over the bogie; the glands, slide-bars, combination lever and valve spindle could then have been reached without difficulty by a man standing on the track between the frame-plates. A Derby design of 1924 for a 3-cylinder compound 4–6–0 had just this layout.

The early history of the Royal Scots shows fortune favouring the brave, for these 50 engines produced in a tremendous hurry to an untried design based on a virtually untried design (Lord Nelson had seen no real service by November 1926) turned out to be better engines than the 16 Nelsons. They ran the 450-ton "Royal Scot" throughout the 1927–28 winter, non-stop between Euston and Carlisle (299 miles), at an average of 52mph (down) and 50.5mph (up).

The record length of the non-stop run was a centre-piece in LMS publicity in 1927–28 and it is in fact an unbroken world's record in respect of a regular train service throughout the winter. A very striking coloured poster gave a vivid artist's impression of a Royal Scot at speed under a stormy sky, and in the act of passing a train running on a parallel line behind what, with some imagination, might be interpreted as a Gresley Pacific, but it is very unlikely that that ever actually happened.

The LMS also published a book written by S. P. B. Mais under the title "*Royal Scot and her forty-nine sisters*". This treated the subject lyrically with appropriate quotations from Kipling and Masefield and included concise comments on the 25 historic locomotives whose names had been copied on Scots Nos 6125 to 6149. Corresponding notes were made about the army regiments after which Nos 6100–6124 were named. These included the one of such repute that it claimed no name but only the reference HLI; this was LMS No 6121.

After the usual initial period of a year or two during which the better enginemen learned the "tricks" of the Royal Scots the engines showed themselves to be well able to do all that was needed on the LMS. They were lively, if not sparkling, and when in good condition, economical. On one dynamometer test indeed a Royal Scot seemed to be burning only 2.66lb of coal per drawbar horsepower hour, thus beating the Great Western Castle 1924 record of 2.83lb. But the dynamometer was afterwards found to be faulty and the true figure for Royal Scots was more like 3.2.

The large smokebox and the very short chimneys of the Royal Scots made them inevitably bad in a manner quite detestable to enginemen. When running with low exhaust pressure, steam and smoke from the chimney were caught up in the vortex of air behind the front edge of the smokebox and escaped from it downwards so that the engine had a built-in front-end fog. No driver likes thus running "blind" even when he is so sure of his road that he can shut off steam in order to see each signal as he passes it. The condition is very risky

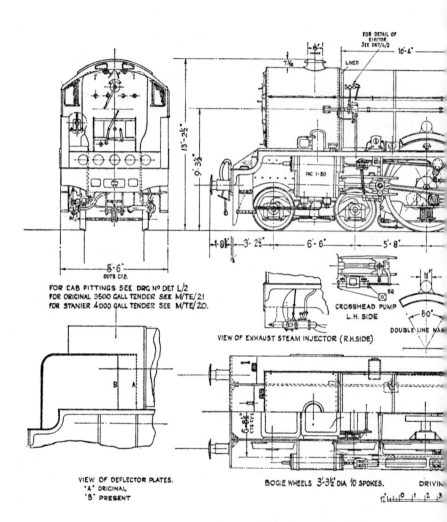

FOR CAB FITTINGS SEE DRG Nº DET L/2
FOR ORIGINAL 3500 GALL TENDER SEE M/TE/21
FOR STANIER 4000 GALL TENDER SEE M/TE/20.

VIEW OF EXHAUST STEAM INJECTOR (R.H.SIDE)

CROSSHEAD PUMP
L.H. SIDE

VIEW OF DEFLECTOR PLATES.
'A' ORIGINAL
'B' PRESENT

BOGIE WHEELS 3'-3½" DIA 10 SPOKES.

The original Fowler/North British Locomotive
Company design for the Royal Scot class of
engines. Drawings for the rebuilt locomotives
appear on pages 56 and 57

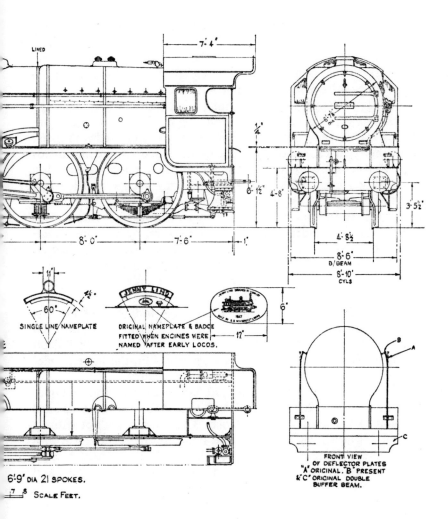

LINED

7'-4"

1½"

6'-1½" 4'-8"

8'-0" 7'-6" 1'

3'-5½"

4'-8½"

8'-6"
B/BEAM

6'-10"
CYLS

6"

11"

2½"

60°

SINGLE LINE NAMEPLATE

DERBY LINE

ORIGINAL NAMEPLATE & BADGE
FITTED WHEN ENGINES WERE
NAMED AFTER EARLY LOCOS.

12"

6'-9" DIA 21 SPOKES.

7   8   SCALE FEET.

FRONT VIEW
OF DEFLECTOR PLATES
"A" ORIGINAL. "B" PRESENT
& "C" ORIGINAL DOUBLE
BUFFER BEAM.

and may well have been the reason why the driver of a Royal Scot ignored a distant signal on his north-bound approach to Leighton Buzzard and thus caused a disastrous high-speed derailment there on Sunday March 22, 1931.

Many varied modifications were made to the top part of Royal Scot smokeboxes in endeavours to dissuade the exhaust from rolling downwards but nothing was found to be so effective as the "smoke-lifting screens" developed in Germany and first used extensively in Britain on Southern Railway King Arthurs.

By 1932 the Royal Scots with multi-ring piston valves were the best main-line passenger engines that the LMS or any of its constituents had ever had and their owners were quite pleased with them. But in that year charge of LMS locomotives passed into the hands of W. A. Stanier who came from the Great Western at Swindon where he had spent all his working life. This background led him to criticise some Royal Scot features. The 70 engines each averaged three failures in two years by overheated axleboxes. This did not surprise Stanier when he saw what were, by Swindon standards, imperfections in the design of the axleboxes. Rectification quickly began and with axleboxes rationally designed, manufactured and fitted, the average Royal Scot averaged only one "hot box" failure in 10 years.

Stanier had commented on the size of the smokebox of the first Royal Scot when it was exhibited rather proudly in 1927 and soon confirmed that, as he suspected, Royal Scot smokeboxes were difficult to keep air-tight after some years of service. Furthermore, boiler repair costs were high by Great Western standards.

So, in 1937, a Royal Scot, No 6170, appeared with a taper-boiler and cylindrical smokebox carried on a saddle formed as an upward extension of the inside-cylinder block. The chassis was not entirely new, but was largely that of the residue of an abortive experiment with a three-boiler, three-pressure, three-cylinder, two-superheater semi-compound locomotive using 900lb/sq in steam that burst a tube and killed a man.

The only real advantage of tapering the barrel of a boiler was a small reduction in weight at the front end, but on the LMS the tapered barrel was an indication that internal details were in a Great Western style that minimised repair costs. The smokebox was so much smaller in diameter than that of the old Scots that there was enough height for a recognisable chimney. The difference in this part of the engine made it unnecessary to fit smoke-lifting plates to No 6170.

The next Royal Scot to be given a taper boiler was No 6103 and this was done during World War II in 1943. The boiler was generally similar to that of No 6170 but was not identical with it. No 6103 had cylinders of a new design and also a double chimney arranged to enable the boiler to be worked harder with a given blast-pipe pressure than was possible with a single chimney.

In her new form No 6103 showed such power and speed that in the course of time all the Royal Scots were similarly "converted". This was the official term but in fact very little of the original Scot appeared in the Converted Scot. Boiler, cylinders and wheel centres were all new and so, in some cases, was the frame. In effect the cab of a Royal Scot was re-erected on a new engine and for accountancy purposes this was a "conversion" of the original Scot.

Apart from difficulty of access to the inside mechanism, the Converted Scots may be claimed to be the best British 4-6-0s. The Great Western four-cylinder 4-6-0s were certainly the previous bests and the advantage of the Converted Scots over them may not in general have been more than marginal but during the "locomotive exchanges" of 1948 the superiority of the Converted Scots over the Great Western Kings was quite marked. When occasion justified it the Scots were "opened out" to produce higher power than the Pacifics usually did during those trials.

Later on the exceptional haulage power of the Converted Scots was occasionally demonstrated in some of the more difficult jobs in ordinary service. Figures relating to some of these are given in the table on page 62.

The use of a boiler pressure as high as 250lb/sq in in the Royal Scots was just to be well up with the fashion-leaders in 1927. Boiler maintenance would have been less expensive with 200lb/sq in and correspondingly larger cylinders, but even without enlarging the cylinders good work could have been obtained from the engines. *Railway World* for August 1960 contains on p229 details of two good runs from Nuneaton to Stafford by a Converted Jubilee and a Converted Scot each hauling 530 tons. The engines were almost identical except that the former had cylinders nominally half an inch smaller in diameter than the other. Both trains passed Milford (32.4 miles) in about 33 minutes and the times differed by only eight seconds. Yet the Converted Jubilee ran with boiler pressure nowhere higher than 180lb/sq in; on the other engine the boiler pressure was not far below the blowing-off figure of 250lb/sq in. The common power-output per square foot of grate area exceeded a "high-class standard" established on the basis of the best efforts of representative classes of all four pre-nationalisation railway groups.

The low exhaust pressure that the double-chimney permitted led to a repetition of the steam-drifting problem and Converted Scots were all eventually fitted with side-sheets alongside the smokebox.

A long-standing trouble with Royal Scots both "old" and "converted" was that of rough riding when things had worn slack. It was of such a type as to persuade drivers to slow down a bit when coming to certain rough places in the track but it might not have bothered enginemen used to the wild riding of Ivatt Atlantics on the LNER. One cannot help wondering whether there would have been less trouble of this kind if the wheel-base of the Lord Nelson had been adopted when the Royal Scots were being designed in 1927.

But even as it was, the riding of Converted Scots was improved by adjustment of side-control springs and friction in the bogie. In normal circumstances they rode safely at any speed they could reach and in their last years they occasionally touched 100mph in ordinary service.

Performance in Service

by JOHN POWELL, CENG, BSc(ENG), MIMECHE

I WOULD hazard a guess that not more than one in five of those who read this book have stood on the footplate of a locomotive in steam. Probably not more than one in 50 have travelled on a steam locomotive in main line service. Let us therefore start by painting a background to locomotive operation.

The average person seriously interested in the steam locomotive tends to dream dreams. Stalwart crews, dedicated to the service of this most fascinating of machines, apply themselves eagerly to reverser and shovel in a crusade against friction and gravity. The firebox backplate becomes a sort of altar before which rituals are performed, coal and water and sweat are offered up, so that mankind can benefit from the expected bounty. The very word footplate, and the mental picture it conjures up, induce thoughts tinged with a rosy glow.

The fascination of the footplate is certainly unchallenged, but to experience it in reality was to have some cherished illusions shattered. It was a crude workplace, dirty, noisy in the extreme, given to lurches and vibration. Cold draughts whistled in to temper burning heat, forward vision was often ludicrous, and every activity and control required real physical effort.

And the men? A minority of them, highly skilled and in tune with the locomotive, could cause its performance to soar above the hum-drum everyday level. But all too many were mediocre, semi-skilled men producing a semi-skilled result, men for whom punctuality called for no particular striving, or heavy-handed thrashers, or men not always interested enough to collect their weekly notices. Studied technique was far from universal, on both sides of the footplate; and the more competent the locomotive, the less meticulously was it developed.

That this was not just a product of World War II may be seen from an account of a 1937 journey from Euston to Carlisle[1] in which a "good but undistinguished" run to Rugby was followed by an electrifying run to Crewe (75.5 miles, 71 minutes net, with No 6133 *The Green Howards* on a 395 ton gross train). "As a suitable set off to any jubilation . . . the fresh set of enginemen that took over the

[1] Cecil J. Allen, *Railway Magazine*, September 1937

29

engine at Crewe succeeded in losing time over practically every section from Crewe to Carlisle *with the same engine*, and after seven minutes going against engine and eight minutes overtime against stations we arrived 15 minutes late".

The steam locomotive was, in general, a remarkably tolerant machine, accepting a variety of treatment and operating style from its handlers with little complaint, only protesting at their worst excesses. Its servicing facilities were almost totally lacking in sophistication. The quality of the raw material of its power would have dismayed the owner of a domestic stove, accustomed to water free from leaves, and graded sizes of fuel.

This is the context within which the operation of any steam locomotive class must be studied. By the very nature of things, most of what has been published in the enthusiast press has been concerned with the top 20 per cent of its performances, about which one could enthuse. The Royal Scots were no exception. Top dogs on the LMS for less than 10 years before being progressively displaced from the hardest turns by the Stanier Pacifics, they nevertheless put up performances, particularly in their rebuilt form, which were little inferior to those of vastly bigger engines. As we became used to Princesses and Duchesses, the Royal Scots came to look modest in size when related to the 15 coach trains that were so often their task and perhaps this very comparison did something to foster the respect with which they were regarded.

Enough of generalities. If we are to look at operation, a look first at the footplate itself is appropriate. The Scots retained the side-window Fowler cab throughout their lives, with a footplate level higher than most of their contemporaries. The usual tip-up wooden seats were fitted, and the weather protection was fairly good except in side-wind driving rain conditions. The cab roof was in two parts, with a detachable extension extending from just in front of the handrail pillars: there was a tendency to leak rain at the joint, and it dripped reliably on to one's neck when seated.

The normal LMS double-handled screw reverse was fitted, with a most inconspicuous pointer against a scale of equally-spaced graduations à la Midland. The important ones were subsequently engraved for 10, 15, 22, 30 and 38 per cent cut-off in forward gear.

In parallel boiler form, the boiler mountings were pure Fowler, with combination clack boxes/injector steam valves, sand and blower valves combined over the sliding firehole door, Midland vacuum/steam brake valve to the driver's right hand (on top of which a folded sponge-cloth often resided) and a Midland pull-handle for the large ejector steam, the actual valve and ejectors being just behind the smokebox on the driver's side. The injector water controls were under the seats, exhaust steam injector being on the right side.

As rebuilt with taper "2A" boiler, the firebox backplate became a mixture of Stanier and Fowler practice. A steam manifold high up under the cab roof carried the injector steam valves and fed brake, ejectors, pressure gauge, whistle and carriage warming, but irrationally the Midland combined sand and blower valve was retained instead of providing the separate Stanier sanding valve on the driver's side. In due course rocking grate controls appeared on the cab floor under the firehole door. Damper controls were never a strong point on the LMS and the "walking-stick" handles coming up through the floor on the fireman's side often needed to be held open with spanners, brick-ends or string.

An interesting feature worth mentioning arose from the unbalanced nature of the regulator handle, which tended to close due to vibration when running. A number of drivers carried with them a flat wooden wedge, about 1½in wide, which they would insert between the handle and the stop on the quadrant, pulling the handle back on to the wedge to hold it. Others, less adept at joinery, would scrutinise the coal for a flat piece of similar size, and this often lived, when not in use, on the tray above the firehole door. It was quite a versatile piece of equipment, because due to the differential action of the regulator when opening and closing[2] the same wedge could give both first valve and a sizable slice of the main valve also.

A brief word on the rocking grate in relation to performance; the whole aim, apart from advantages during fire cleaning on the shed, was that they should be used regularly on the journey, say every 25 miles, to rock out the ash as it formed and before it could fuse into large slabs of clinker which so seriously interfere with air flow through the firebed. They would have been a god-send on the road, but to be so would have needed to be 100 per cent reliable; they were not—only 98 per cent. That was that: if men were in dire trouble with the fire, they would reluctantly rock the grate because it could not make the situation worse, no matter what happened. But if things were tolerable, better to carry on that way than risk either a broken grate section, or the grate jammed in the rocked position by a piece of clinker, or skinned knuckles because the detachable handle was a poor fit on the operating stub. Use of rocking grates were confined almost entirely to disposal duties on the shed, and this was not confined to the Royal Scots, but was quite general.

[2] *Railway Magazine*, January 1951

Also worthy of comment is the tender front. The Stanier 4000 gallon tender continued the later Midland practice of folding doors to give access to the coal space, with a gap about 12in deep below them for the normal coal feed, on to the shovelling plate. Well, it all depended on the coal of course, If you got a tenderful of hard Yorkshire at Camden, it was liable to be big slabs which needed a lot of pick work to break up to come out through the opening— you daren't open the doors, at least in the early stages of a run, otherwise you'd have been deluged in coal. On the other hand, if you had a high proportion of cobbles and small coal, you were ankle deep in the stuff for the first hour or more. And in conditions like that men will put more into the box than is strictly necessary, just to clear their feet.

As on most other LMS engines, injectors left a lot to be desired. The exhaust injectors were not too bad for reliability—the operating linkage was reasonably direct and the live steam/exhaust changeover valves didn't get the hammering on long distance express work that they did on, say, the 'Crabs' on local freight. The live steam injectors, real relics of Midland practice, were poor starters and you could soon be in trouble to maintain the boiler if the exhaust injector wouldn't do its stuff. No doubt this conditioned the men to run, as they did, with water bobbing in the top nut of the gauge.

The preparation of a Scot was fairly straightforward, but like all the 3-cylinder LMS 4-6-0s, the divided drive put the inside cylinder forward over the leading bogie axle, and so the crosshead, little end and combination lever came nicely over the bogie centre casting, in a space confined by the inside motion plate and the exhaust steam pipes from the outside cylinders. Not the choicest place to do the oiling, particularly since the bogie casting became a receptacle for all the spilt oil, muck and leakage water. Many drivers entrusted this part of the job to their more agile firemen, and many were the old overall jackets kept specially for this chore.

The Royal Scots, both in parallel- and taper-boiler form, could be driven quite happily with wide-open regulator and short cutoffs. The valve setting of the taper-boiler engines, within the limits of the old combination levers, called for $1\frac{3}{8}$in lap and $\frac{5}{16}$in lead, and this long lead on 9in valves for 18in cylinders, gave very large port openings at short cutoffs. This produced extremely "punchy" performance at cutoffs of the order of 15 per cent. Indeed, indicator tests made on No 6138, an early conversion, showed indicated horsepowers as high as 946 at 6 per cent cutoff at 60mph. Equally, the first valve of the regulator, giving 130–140lb /sq in in the steamchest, with rather longer cutoffs, appeared to give equally satisfactory results, and certainly gave a softer exhaust which minimised spark throwing at the chimney.

In practice, most Western Division men stuck to the first valve of the regulator when they could get away with it—and the "limited load" timings could be maintained quite happily this way except on the steeper banks—and opened on to the second valve only for the faster timings. Full regulator work was comparatively rare on the West Coast main line, though Scottish and Midland men indulged in it rather more.

The parallel boiler engines were remarkably free from slipping for an engine of their power, with an adhesion factor of no more than 4.22. Despite the reduced weight and a factor reduced to 4.13, the taper boiler rebuilds were also very good, but there was a certain amount of trouble with slipping at high speeds—other classes have had similar trouble—and consequent bending of coupling rods. It was in an attempt to mitigate this that additional sandboxes were provided on the platform to give forward sand to the trailing coupled wheels.

The grates on original and rebuilt Scots were very similar in form, being about 9ft 6in long with the front 7ft or so inclined at about 1 in 5 and the rear portion level. The ashpans had front and back dampers, and at one time also intermediate dampers in the hump over the trailing coupled axle, though these were seldom used. If the front damper were opened, quite a brisk combustion was induced at the front of the grate, and this increased the fireman's work appreciably. The drill was therefore, to run with only the back damper fully open, and to concentrate the firing on the back half of the grate.

With coal consumption invariably in the 40-50lb per mile range, depending on speeds and loads, most firemen adopted a modified "little and often" technique: after all, the official teaching of six to eight shovels at a time would have looked a bit lost on a grate of that size. So it was common practice to fire about 12 shovelsful at a time, say two in each of the back corners, about three down each side to the half-way mark, and a couple inside the door. This maintained a slightly hollow fire at the back, usually to just above the bottom of the firehole, and kept part-burnt coal gravitating down the slope of the grate to sustain an even, thinnish fire at the front. Any preponderance of small stuff was kept for inside the firehole, where the draught would take it off the shovel and spread it lightly, or, if caked, could readily be opened up by a bit of digging with the shovel. Fired this way, the Scots would steam their heads off, with the firehole

D

doors open much of the time to avoid blowing off. Besides, it was easy work for the fireman, for there was little need for coal at the front unless the fire became uneven.

There were those, of course, who believed in putting on 25 or 30 at a time, with longer sit-downs in between. Usually this meant a thicker fire pretty well up to the underside of the firehole deflector plate, not well burnt through at the back, and such firemen were involved in a lot of pushing and prodding with the shovel to make room for fresh coal; indeed, the whole thing worked rather like a coking plant at the back of the grate, the burning and partly coked fuel being pushed and shaken forward to complete combustion. It was a passably satisfactory way of firing, and did not cause smoke except when the regulator was shut, but it certainly produced no better results and appeared to add to the fireman's labours.

In their early days the parallel-boiler Royal Scots could vary from brilliant to very indifferent performers. In the former field we saw some fine exploits in high speed and long distance running, for instance, on April 27, 1928, No 6113 *Cameronian*, on a special nine-coach Glasgow portion of the down "Royal Scot" designed to steal the thunder of the start of non-stop running by the LNER between Kings Cross and Edinburgh, worked non-stop over the 401.4 miles from Euston to Glasgow, taking 488 minutes as compared with the easy 495 minute schedule. Coal consumption, excluding shed duties, was 41.9lb mile. Similarly, No 6127 *Novelty*, less than three months later, worked a special train from Glenboig to Euston (395.8 miles) non-stop with an 11-coach train.

Then there were the high-speed special trains run between Euston and Coventry for the Humber-Hillman-Commer Company on September 19 and 20, 1933. Cecil J. Allen[3] commented:

". . . although no tighter times than 90 minutes down and 88 minutes up had been laid down for the 92 mile journey, drivers had been given a fairly free hand as to running ahead of schedule. As a result, engine No 6129 *Comet*, with a light load of seven coaches weighing 212 tons gross, came up from Coventry to Euston in 79min 1 sec, notwithstanding a dead stand for signals on Camden bank and a couple of slight checks earlier in the run. Tremendous speeds were made—90mph before Weedon, 80 minimum at Roade, 92 at Castlethorpe, a minimum of 82 through Cheddington before the first signal check, 90 at Kings Langley and 91½ at Wembley. From Welton to Willesden

$69\frac{3}{4}$ miles were covered in 50min 53sec or very little over 49 minutes net, at an average of just over 85mph. Marchant and Aldridge were the driver and fireman respectively.

Even more meritorious, in view of a much heavier load of 335 tons (11 coaches) was the feat of Driver J. Jones and Fireman Charge in making a net time of 77 minues; on this latter trip the $69\frac{3}{4}$ miles from Welton to Willesden occupied 51min 47sec . . . which involved an average speed of 80.8mph for this distance. In the reverse direction, the best time with the 335 ton train was . . . made by Earl; notwithstanding a loss of two minutes by signals after Tring, Rugby, $82\frac{1}{2}$ miles, was passed in 76min 3sec, and Coventry was reached in 87min 8sec, or 85 minutes net."

But the Achilles heel of the Scots at this time was the piston valves The original valve heads, with a single broad ring, allowed a lot of steam leakage as wear took place, and coal consumption rose substantially. On unspecified classes fitted with this type of valve head a rise of up to 80 per cent in coal consumption prior to valve examinations was recorded. The conversion to multiple narrow-ring valve heads in the early Stanier régime put a stop to this once and for all, and thereafter all the 3-cylinder 4–6–0s would go the full 36,000 miles—often further—between examinations with negligible wear. Atomised lubrication was also a significant factor. This more than any of the other modifications to axleboxes, bogies, etc, turned them into a footplate man's machine of first class.

The taper boiler rebuilds brought a number of additional benefits:

a) the boiler and gas flow proportions
which, apart from some mis-proportioning of the small tubes ($1\frac{7}{8}$in diameter tubes would have been preferable to the $1\frac{3}{4}$in diameter tubes used), gave a much better balance in free gas areas between superheater flues and small tubes.[4]

[4] Parallel boilers:

27 flues $5\frac{1}{8}$in OD $\times$7swg, $1\frac{1}{2}$in elements   A/S ratio $\frac{1}{530}$

180 tubes 2in OD $\times$11swg   A/S ratio $\frac{1}{352}$

Free gas areas: Large tubes 2.03sq ft
                 Small tubes 3.07sq ft

                 Total 5.10sq ft = 16.3% grate area.

Taper boilers:

28 flues $5\frac{1}{8}$in OD $\times$7swg, $1\frac{1}{4}$in elements   A/S ratio $\frac{1}{360}$

198 tubes $1\frac{3}{4}$in OD $\times$12swg   A/S ratio $\frac{1}{410}$

Free gas areas: Large tubes 2.52sq ft
                 Large tubes 2.56sq ft

                 Total 5.08sq ft = 16.3% grate area.

b) the double blastpipe and chimney
   which successfully extended the "front end limit" of output
   of the boiler.
c) the general front end design
   with generous, internally streamlined steam and exhaust
   passages better able to pass high steam volumes with
   minimum resistance.

The effect of these changes was to push maximum service drawbar
horsepowers from about 1500 with the parallel boiler engines to
about 1700 in their rebuilt form.

With my extensive footplate experience confined to the post-
World War II years, I saw comparatively little of the parallel-boilered
Royal Scots from the footplate, and such journeys as I did have with
them were unspectacular and do not warrant inclusion here.

Inevitably it is to Cecil J. Allen's articles in the *Railway Magazine*
during 1936–1939 that one must now look for an insight into the best
of their daily work. This was the period of the LMS "On Time"
campaign, allied with the steady introduction of faster schedules, and
footplate and operating staffs were encouraged by punctuality news
sheets, competitions and publicity; footplate morale was at a high
level. The worst effects of the depression on deferred maintenance
had been overcome, staff shortage was non-existent, and the Pacifics
were not yet present in sufficient numbers to do more than cream
off a few of the harder turns.

From the chronicles of this period I have selected three runs to
illustrate something of what was expected of the Royal Scots, and of
how they rose to the occasion.

Table 1 is a long non-stop run from Carlisle to Euston on the
Aberdeen and Edinburgh portion of the up "Royal Scot", on a mile-
a-minute schedule with a moderate load of 11 coaches. The impressive
feature of this run, to me, is not the peak levels of power output,
respectable as these were, but the sustained level of output throughout
the journey, indicating excellent management by Fireman Spencer.
On the 1 in 125 from Thrimby Grange up to Shap No 6132 was
producing 1200 equivalent DBHP, accelerating from a minimum of
37 to a sustained 40mph. From being on time through Preston,
checks through the industrial belt of Lancashire brought the train
to a maximum lateness of 11 minutes at Coppenhall Junction, north
of Crewe, and Driver Brooker set about achieving a punctual arrival
with all the skill that he was to exhibit, 10 years later, with No 46164
on the Locomotive Interchange Trials of 1948. He had no more than

TABLE 1—UP ROYAL SCOT (ABERDEEN & EDINBURGH PORTION)

Locomotive: No 6132 *The King's Regiment, Liverpool*
Load: 11 bogies, 339 tons tare, 355 tons gross
Driver: F. Brooker   Fireman: W. Spencer (Camden)

Distance miles		Schedule min	Actual Time min sec		Speed mph
0.0	CARLISLE	0	0	00	—
4.9	Wreay		9	47	40
7.4	Southwaite		13	05	48/52
10.8	Calthwaite		17	07	50
13.1	Plumpton	19	19	52	57/60
17.9	PENRITH	24	24	48	54/62½
20.6	mp 48½		27	28	60½
26.1	mp 43		34	45	37
28.1	mp 41		38	01	40
29.5	Shap		39	52	47
31.5	Shap Summit	41	42	32	45
37.0	TEBAY	46	47	07	82/80½
43.1	Grayrigg		52	07	66
50.0	OXENHOLME	58	58	12	77
55.5	Milnthorpe		62	11	86½
59.6	mp 9½		65	09	76
62.8	CARNFORTH	69	67	39	82
69.1	LANCASTER	74	73	35	62½
70.2	Lancaster No 1		74	47	46½
74.9	Bay Horse		79	47	67
80.6	Garstang	85	84	45	72½
85.4	Barton		88	57	64½
90.1	PRESTON	95	94	50	25*
			pw and signal slacks		
141.1	CREWE	148	158	32	slack*
145.8	Betley Road		164	51	54/53
151.6	Whitmore	161	171	06	64½
155.7	Standon Bridge		174	35	79
			sigs.		50
160.3	Norton Bridge		178	51	64½
165.6	STAFFORD	174	183	27	75/45*
175.0	RUGELEY	183	192	30	80½/77
182.9	LICHFIELD	190	198	30	82/86½
189.1	TAMWORTH	195	203	07	82
196.8	Atherstone		209	05	73
202.0	NUNEATON	207	213	07	81
205.7	Bulkington		216	09	70½
216.6	RUGBY	222	225	18	81/38*
220.4	Kilsby Tunnel N		229	58	56
223.9	Welton		233	26	68
229.5	Weedon		237	46	83½
236.4	BLISWORTH	240	242	56	79
239.3	Roade	243	245	16	72½
244.4	Castlethorpe		248	58	88
246.7	Wolverton		250	39	85½
252.5	BLETCHLEY	254	255	02	79
259.0	Leighton Buzzard		260	12	74
263.1	Cheddington		263	39	69
267.5	TRING	268	267	36	64
271.2	Berkhamsted		270	47	75
278.2	Kings Langley		276	10	82
281.7	WATFORD JUNCTION	280	278	50	77½
			eased		
293.8	WILLESDEN JUNCTION	291	290	27	69
299.2	EUSTON	299	298	33	—
		Net time: 287½min			

* permanent speed restriction

151 minutes allowed for the 158.1 miles from Crewe to Euston. To sustain 53mph up the 1 in 177 to Madeley called for 1320 EDBHP and the fine climb to Tring, after 4½ hours steaming, was a result of still being able to sustain 1220 EDBHP. Net time for the 299.2 miles from Carlisle was no more than 287½ minutes. Little wonder that Cecil J. Allen[5] commenting on this run, could say:

"It is clear that there is still plenty of life in the Royal Scots which, when in good condition, are doing better than ever."

Next comes a run[6] by No 6166 *London Rifle Brigade* on the heavy "Mancunian" between Wilmslow and Euston on a 61.7mph "Special

TABLE 2—UP MANCUNIAN, MANCHESTER–EUSTON
Locomotive: No 6166 *London Rifle Brigade*
Load: 15 coaches, 466 tons tare, 500 tons gross. (Special Limit Timings, 415 tons allowed)
Driver: Not stated

Distance miles							Schedule min	Actual Time min sec		Speed mph
0.0	WILMSLOW	..	..	..	..	..	0	0	00	—
8.5	Goostrey	..	..	..	..	..		11	22	—
14.3	Sandbach	..	..	..	..	..	15	16	18	71½
								pws		30
18.8	CREWE	..	..	..	..	..	21	22	42	30*
23.6	Betley Road	..	..	..	..			29	31	47½
26.8	Madeley	..	..	..	..			33	40	45
29.3	Whitmore	..	..	..	..	..	34	36	49	—
33.5	Standon Bridge		..	..	..			40	43	71½
								sigs		50
38.0	Norton Bridge	..	..	..	..		42	44	52	72½
43.3	STAFFORD	..	..	..	..		47	49	33	40*
52.6	RUGELEY	..	..	..	..			59	38	70½
60.6	LICHFIELD	..	..	..	..		63	66	44	65
66.9	TAMWORTH	..	..	..	..			72	02	74
								pws		
70.4	Polesworth	..	..	..	..			75	30	—
79.8	NUNEATON	..	..	..	..		82	84	41	64½
83.4	Bulkington	..	..	..	..			88	10	60
94.3	RUGBY	..	..	..	..		95	98	15	70½/48*
98.1	Kilsby Tunnel N	..	..	..				—		54
107.2	Weedon	..	..	..	..			111	03	75
114.1	BLISWORTH	..	..	..	..			116	51	—
117.0	Roade	..	..	..	..		116	119	31	62½
124.5	Wolverton	..	..	..	..			125	49	74
130.2	BLETCHLEY	..	..	..	..		127	131	08	—
136.6	Leighton Buzzard	..	..	..	..			137	01	—
140.8	Cheddington	..	..	..	..			140	47	—
145.2	TRING	..	..	..	..		141	145	21	55½
152.4	Hemel Hempstead	..	..	..				151	39	76½
159.5	WATFORD JUNCTION		..	..				157	09	77½
165.5	Harrow	..	..	..	..			162	08	75
171.5	WILLESDEN JUNCTION		..	..		164	167	06	60*
176.9	EUSTON	..	..	..	..		172	173	49	—

* permanent speed restriction   Net time: 171min

[5] *Railway Magazine*, August 1939
[6] *Railway Magazine*, September 1936

TABLE 3—CARLISLE–SYMINGTON

Locomotive: No 6113 Cameronian
Load: 12 coaches, 375 tons tare, 395 tons gross
Driver: Not stated

Distance miles		Schedule min	Actual Time min sec		Speed mph
0.0	CARLISLE	0	0	00	—
4.1	Rockcliffe		7	12	—
	Floriston			—	62
8.6	Gretna	11	11	55	—
13.0	Kirkpatrick		17	38	45½
16.7	Kirtlebridge	20	22	01	—
20.1	Ecclefechan		25	35	—
22.7	Castlemilk..		28	39	45½
25.8	LOCKERBIE	30	31	40	—
28.7	Nethercleugh		34	13	71
34.5	Wamphray		39	46	68
39.7	BEATTOCK..	44	44	53	58½
42.3	Auchencastle		48	02	38½
45.4	Greskine		53	47	30
47.8	Harthope		58	16	33
49.7	Beattock Summit	64	61	52	33½
52.6	Elvanfoot		64	48	—
57.8	Abington		69	10	76
66.9	SYMINGTON	81	78	35	—

Limit" schedule (Table 2). The 15-coach train was 51 tons over the limit set for this timing, and consequently the task was very near the upper limit of what the parallel-boiler engines could tackle. Quite early checks costing 2¾ minutes precluded a right-time arrival, but the work done was very fine, without depending on any very high speeds downhill. The climb to Whitmore, with no lower speed than 45 topping the 1 in 177 at Madeley, was particularly good with this load, and the surprisingly high figure of 60 minimum at Bulkington should be noted also. The minimum of 55½ over Tring was first-class: equivalent DBHPs were 1425 at Madeley and 1330 at Tring Cutting, and net time overall was only 171 minutes.

By comparison, another Scot on the 4.10pm Manchester–Euston[7] did even better up to Whitmore. Laurie Earl of Camden, with No 6125 on a lighter train of 375 tons gross, passed Whitmore in no more than 14min 35sec from the start at Crewe (10.5 miles), having sustained 52½mph on the 1 in 177 to Madeley; this called for something like 1510EDBHP. Subsequent work was not quite to this standard, however.

Finally, a run northwards on the Caledonian main line from Carlisle is reproduced in Table 3 from a pre-war Cecil J. Allen article[8] to show the highest power output that I have been able to trace from information published about these engines. In the early stages, No

[7] Railway Magazine, October 1939
[8] Railway Magazine, March 1936

6113 *Cameronian* seems to have been held in to the point of dropping time on a not difficult schedule—perhaps it came on cold at Carlisle, though this was not stated—and it was not until after Lockerbie that the engine was really given its head to make a remarkable climb to Beattock Summit. Mr Allen commented at the time:

"An average of 41.2mph up the 15.2 miles from Wamphray to Summit . . . must, one imagines, be extremely rare here for a 4–6–0 locomotive hauling all but 400 tons of train . . ."

After falling to 30mph on the bank at Greskine, the engine was opened out further and accelerated steadily to 33 at Harthope and

TABLE 4—DOWN LANCASTRIAN, 6.0 pm EUSTON–MANCHESTER

Locomotive: No 6170 *British Legion*
Load: 13 coaches, 415 tons tare, 445 tons gross
Driver: Not stated

Distance miles		Schedule min	Actual Time min sec	Speed mph
0.0	EUSTON	0	0 00	—
5.4	WILLESDEN JUNCTION	9	9 10†	62
8.1	Wembley		11 50	61½
11.4	Harrow		15 05	61
13.3	Hatch End		16 59	60
17.5	WATFORD JUNCTION	21	21 00	67
			pws	
24.5	Hemel Hempstead		32 43	15
31.7	TRING	36	43 21	56
40.2	Leighton Buzzard		50 17	82¼
46.7	BLETCHLEY	48	55 07	77
52.4	Wolverton		59 30	82
59.9	Roade	60	65 48	65
62.8	BLISWORTH	63	68 23	76
			sigs	
69.7	Weedon		75 53	60
75.3	Welton		81 26	62¼
80.3	Hillmorton		85 51	76
82.6	RUGBY	81	88 43	40*
91.3	Shilton		98 11	70½/66½
97.1	NUNEATON	95	103 00	81
110.0	TAMWORTH	108	113 04	—
116.3	LICHFIELD	113	118 08	66¼
124.3	RUGELEY	*20	124 56	78
129.5	Milford		129 16	72
133.6	STAFFORD	130	133 03	56*
138.9	Norton Bridge	136	138 48	59
147.6	Whitmore	145	147 12	64
150.2	Madeley		149 30	74
155.8	Basford Sand Sdgs		153 40	85
158.1	CREWE	156	156 53	15*
			pws	
162.6	Sandbach	162	167 39	—
175.2	Alderley Edge		181 48	68¼
176.9	WILMSLOW	176	184 05	—

Net time: 166min

* Permanent speed restriction   † Banked in rear to Camden

$33\frac{1}{2}$ at Summit. This required no less than 1590EDBHP. No doubt the boiler was mortgaged somewhat to produce this output, but the subsequent speed of 76 at Crawford shows that *Cameronian* was not so winded that she had to be coasted down into the Clyde Valley.

The rebuild of the ill-fated water tube boiler engine *Fury* was a sort of intermediate stage between the original Scots and the taper-boiler rebuilds. The boiler proportions were generally good, though being longer between tube-plates the tube ratios were somewhat less than ideal: the front end was similar in style to the rebuilds, but of course until after the war with a single blastpipe and chimney.

I have only been able to trace a single published run with this engine in this form, made in 1938 on the 6.0pm Euston–Manchester train, the "Lancastrian", non-stop at 60.3mph average to Wilmslow[9]. Table 4 gives the details of this fine performance, made on a 445 ton train. The sustained 60mph on the rising 1 in 339 past Hatch End called for 1375EDBHP, while the acceleration from the Stafford slack to 64 at Whitmore bettered this slightly, requiring 1390EDBHP. To average 67.7mph net over the 150.4 miles from Willesden to Basford Sand Sidings, Crewe with this load was in the finest tradition of these remarkable 4–6–0s.

As a sort of base "norm" for the rebuilt engines I would first like to repeat details of a run I had on the footplate of No 46164 *The Artists Rifleman* in 1954, already published[10]. At that time, I think the Edge Hill top link was probably the finest collection of enginemen on the Western Division, and the late Maurice Corbett was very much in the top bracket. Having said that, it was not until I came to restudy this performance for the purposes of this book that I came to appreciate just how fine it was. For instance, the sustained 49mph on the 1 in 177 to Madeley required as much as 1580EDBHP, and the 64mph minimum over Tring very little less, about 1500EDBHP. This made it quite clear to me that, far from being done on the first valve of the regulator, as I said at the time, Corbett must have opened out on to the second valve for the climb to Tring while my attention was distracted, and in the absence of a steam chest pressure gauge it escaped my notice. The speeds suggest that this happened in the vicinity of Sears Crossing, and I have accordingly corrected Table 5 from the original published version. This sort of thing could readily happen, and as mentioned earlier, the regulator handle position did not give the game away. The water consumption should be particularly noted: based on the results with these engines during the Interchange

[9] *Railway Magazine*, December 1960
[10] The Lively Royal Scots, by "4567", *Trains Illustrated*, October 1959

TABLE 5—2.10 pm LIVERPOOL LIME STREET—EUSTON

Locomotive: No 46164 *The Artists' Rifleman*
Load: 13 coaches, 414 tons, tare 445 tons gross
(Special Limit timings, 450 tons allowed to Weaver Junction, 475 tons forward to Euston)
Driver: M. Corbett   *Fireman:* S. Walls (Edge Hill)

Distance miles		Schedule min	Actual Time min sec	Speed mph	Regulator	Cut off
0.0	LIVERPOOL LIME ST ..	0	0 00	—	FV	60
1.4	Edge Hill	4	4 24	22	½	25
2.5	Wavertree		6 36	34*	,,	22/30
6.4	Speke Junction ..		10 35	67/63	Shut	—
10.6	Ditton Junction	15	14 06	68	Full	15
13.0	RUNCORN		16 28	54	,,	20
16.1	Sutton Weaver		—	48	Shut	—
19.3	Weaver Junction ..	25	23 10	64/53*	FV	18
	Engine worked lightly to Winsford—priming					
26.8	Winsford Junction ..	32	31 23	52	½	18
32.8	Coppenhall Junction ..	38	37 23	64	Shut	—
			sigs, slight			
35.6	CREWE	42	40 23	28*	3/5	28/18
40.3	Betley Road		47 26	51	,,	22
			sigs, slight			
43.5	Madeley		51 18	49	,,	18
46.0	Whitmore	56	53 55	52	FV	,,
54.8	Norton Bridge	64	61 30	75/71	,,	,,
60.1	STAFFORD	70	66 06	75/58*	,,	,,
	Deliberately slow recovery to Milford					
66.5	Colwich		73 03	62	,,	,,
70.3	RUGELEY	80	75 38	70	,,	,,
77.4	LICHFIELD	87	82 25	73/69	Shut	—
			pws			
	Hademore		—	76/25	FV	22
83.6	TAMWORTH	93	90 11	57	,,	18
91.3	Atherstone		98 08	61/60	,,	16
96.5	NUNEATON	107	102 55	68	,,	,,
102.2	Shilton		108 41	59/62	Shut	—
	Coasting to avoid too early arrival					
110.5	Rugby No 7		pws	25	—	
111.1	RUGBY	124	120 40	—		
0.0		0	0 00	—	3/5	30/18
2.3	Hillmorton		3 41	45	,,	22
7.3	Welton		10 19	52/64	FV	16
12.8	Weedon	14	14 56	78	,,	,,
19.7	BLISWORTH	21	20 28	75	,,	,,
22.6	Roade	24	23 02	67	FV	16
27.8	Castlethorpe		27 08	78	,,	,,
30.1	Wolverton		28 58	77	,,	,,
35.9	BLETCHLEY	36	33 40	72/73	,,	,,
42.3	Leighton Buzzard ..		39 10	70/71	,,	,,
44.4	Sears Crossing		40 55	72	3/5	20
46.4	Cheddington		42 38	69	,,	,,
48.6	Tring Cutting		44 32	65	,,	22
50.9	TRING	52	46 38	64	FV	16
54.6	Berkhamsted		50 01	73	Shut	—
			sigs, block failure			
58.1	Hemel Hempstead		55 05	1	FV	40/16
65.1	WATFORD JUNCTION	65	63 53	66	,,	16
			pws	20	3/5	30/16

71.1	Harrow	..	..	..	71 45	64	FV	16
74.5	Wembley	..	..	..	74 32	76	Shut	—
77.2	WILLESDEN JUNCTION		76	76 42	—	—	—
					sigs		
82.5	EUSTON	..	..	..	84	83 55	—

Net times:
      Liverpool—Rugby 114½min
      Rugby—Euston 75¾min
Water consumption: 6,500 gall—33.6 gall/mile
*Permanent speed restriction. FV: first valve of regulator

TABLE 6—10.0 am BLACKPOOL CENTRAL—EUSTON

Locomotive: 46168 The Girl Guide
Load: 15 bogies, 491 tons tare, 520 tons gross
Driver: Not recorded

Distance miles					Schedule	Actual Time min sec	Speed mph	Regulator	Cut off
0.0	CREWE	..	..	..	0	0 00	—	FV/½	35/30
4.8	Betley Road	..	..			8 32	48	½	30
8.0	Madeley	..				12 48	47	,,	,,
10.5	Whitmore	..	..		16	15 38	50	,,	16
14.7	Standon Bridge	..				19 36	69	FV	,,
19.2	Norton Bridge	..			24	23 33	66	,,	,,
						sigs			
24.5	STAFFORD	..		..arr	31	30 21	—	—	—

0.0	,,	..	..	..dep	0	0 00	—	FV/½	30/25
4.1	Milford	..	..	..	6	—	56	½	20
6.4	Colwich	..	..	..		9 05	63	,,	15
9.3	RUGELEY	..	..	..	11	11 45	68/66	,,	,,
17.3	LICHFIELD	..	..	..	19	18 56	69/64	,,	,,
23.6	TAMWORTH	..	..	..	25	24 26	71/65	,,	,,
27.1	Polesworth	..	..	..		27 37	60/62	2/5	,,
31.3	Atherstone	..	..			32 00	57	,,	,,
36.5	NUNEATON	..	..	..	39	37 35	63/57	,,	,,
42.3	Shilton	..	..	..		44 17	51/53	,,	,,
45.5	Brinklow	..	..	..		47 27	64	,,	,,
50.4	Rugby No 7	..	..			sigs	65/20		
51.0	RUGBY	..	..	..	55	54 30	—	½	22
53.3	Hillmorton	..	..			57 59	43	½	22
54.8	Kilsby Tunnel N ..		..			59 59	47	,,	,,
57.3	Welton	..	..	..		63 57	—	,,	15
63.9	Weedon	..	..	..		69 01	73	,,	,,
						sigs			
81.2	Wolverton	..	..	..		94 50	25	2/5	22
86.9	BLETCHLEY	..	..	..	96	102 33	61	,,	,,
93.3	Leighton Buzzard	..	..			110 47	64	,,	,,
97.5	Cheddington	..	..			112 34	67/65	,,	,,
101.9	TRING	..	..	..	113	117 59	58	,,	15
105.6	Berkhamsted	..	..			120 30	70	Shut	—
						sigs diverted to slow line			
116.1	WATFORD JUNCTION				126	138 38	15		
						sigs slight			
128.2	WILLESDEN JUNCTION				137	153 12	—		
133.6	EUSTON	..	..	..	146	159 44	—		

Net times: Crew-Stafford 30min
          Stafford-Euston .. 130min
Water consumption: 6,450 gall—40.8 gall/mile

Trials this is equivalent to a coal consumption of about 45lb/mile.

Another of my footplate trips on the West Coast main line, not previously published, involved some very fine uphill work, but was subject to serious delays from Rugby southwards. The engine was No 46168 *The Girl Guide*, on a heavy 15-coach train in March 1953, the 10.0am Blackpool Central–Euston. Table 6 gives the details.

With this load, the engine had to be driven rather harder than No 46164 in the previous table, and with half regulator out of Crewe there would be about 210lb in the steamchest on the climb to Whitmore. With 30 per cent cutoff, speed fell on the 1 in 177 no more than from 48–47mph, equivalent to 1550DBHP on the level. To sustain 64–69 on the slight undulations between Rugeley and Elmhurst was good, if less spectacular, running. The other point of real interest is the climb to Tring, with a clear road after major signal checks at Castlethorpe and Wolverton. Speed was still falling slightly at Tring, and EDBHP was thus a little less than the 1630 which a sustained 58 would imply. The net overall running time was 160 minutes, with the Stafford stop, and with 520 tons and the effect of recovery from delays this required a water consumption considerably higher, at 40.8 gallons/mile, than the previous run.

The route on which the rebuilt Royal Scots first made their name, even during war-time, was the Midland one from Leeds to Carlisle, and thence forward over the G&SW line to Glasgow St Enoch. It is therefore appropriate that two of the highest power outputs published

TABLE 7—10.35 am LEEDS CITY—GLASGOW

Locomotive: 46117 *Welsh Guardsman*
Load: 8 coaches, 265 tons tare, 280 tons gross
Driver: Not stated

Distance miles						Schedule min	Actual Time min sec		Speed mph
0.0	HELLIFIELD	..	..	..	..	0	0	00	—
3.2	Settle Junction	..	..	..	..	5	4	37	71
5.2	Settle	..	..	..	..		6	18	61¼
9.6	Helwith Bridge	..	..	..	..		11	19	53
11.2	Horton	..	..	..	..		13	06	54
13.5	Selside	..	..	..	..		15	42	55
15.9	Ribblehead	..	..	..	..		18	29	53½
17.2	Blea Moor	..	..	..	..	27	19	51	52½
22.1	Dent	..	..	..	..	..		24	49	63½
25.4	Garsdale	..	..	..	..		27	42	72½
28.4	Ais Gill	..	..	..	..	40	30	42	52¼
							eased		
35.3	Kirkby Stephen	..	..	..	..		37	13	66
38.5	Crosby Garrett	..	..	..	..		40	07	61½
43.5	Ormside	..	..	..	..		44	52	62¼
46.0	APPLEBY	..	..	..	..	58	48	35	—

with these engines should have involved the ascents to Blea Moor and Ais Gill.

Table 7 records a remarkable north-bound run in 1959 on the 10.35am Leeds–Glasgow train[11]. The engine was No 46117 *Welsh Guardsman*, a Holbeck stalwart since its conversion, with a light train of eight coaches, 280 tons gross. An unprecedented climb to Blea Moor was made, with speed never falling below 52½mph on the 1 in 100, and smart running over the tableland to Ais Gill put the train 9¼ minutes up on schedule by that point. A very leisurely run was therefore made down to Appleby, but with normal speeds "even time" could have been achieved by Ormside (after that climb!) and an arrival in 46½ minutes achieved. Equivalent DBHP on the climb, even with the light train, was 1650.

In the reverse direction, Table 8 records a run with another Holbeck engine, No 46113 *Cameronian*, on the 10.5am "Waverley"

TABLE 8—UP WAVERLEY, 10.5 am EDINBURGH—ST PANCRAS

Locomotive: 46113 *Cameronian*
Load: 9 coaches, 312 tons tare, 335 tons gross (XL Limit timings)
Driver: Not stated

Distance miles						Schedule min	Actual Time min sec		Speed mph
0.0	CARLISLE ..	..	..	..	..	0	0	00	—
0.9	Petteril Bridge Junction		..	..		2	34	—
3.9	Cumwhinton	..	..	..	..		7	18	42
6.8	Cotehill ..	..	..	..	..		10	52	53/69
10.0	Armathwaite	..	..	..	..		13	53	66/71
13.1	mp 295 ..	..	..	..			—	67
15.5	Lazonby ..	..	..	..	..	19	18	31	76
18.4	Little Salkeld	..	..	..	..		20	43	80
19.8	Langwathby	..	..	..	..		21	52	70
23.4	Culgaith ..	..	..	..	..		24	47	73
27.9	Long Marton	..	..	..	..		28	40	67
30.8	APPLEBY ..	..	..	..	..	37	31	48	—
0.5	Ormside	..	..	..	..		3	49	60
							pws		20
7.5	Crosby Garrett		..	..	..		10	33	53/57
10.7	Kirkby Stephen	..	..	..	..		14	07	50/52
14.0	Mallerstang	..	..	..	..		18	05	48/54
17.6	Ais Gill ..	..	..	..	..	24	22	12	48
							pws		25
20.6	Garsdale ..	..	..	..	..		26	18	—
23.8	Dent ..	..	..	..	..		29	57	59
28.7	Blea Moor	..	..	..	..	35	34	44	65
							pws		20
30.0	Ribblehead ..	..	..	..	..		36	50	40
34.8	Horton ..	..	..	..	..		41	33	68
40.8	Settle ..	..	..	..	..		46	35	75
42.7	Settle Junction	..	..	..	..	47	48	06	77
46.0	HELLIFIELD	..	..	..	..	51	52	01	—

Net time: 47min

[11] *Trains Illustrated*, April 1960

from Edinburgh to St Pancras, accelerated at that time south of Carlisle to "XL Limit" timings[12]. A late start from Carlisle provided the incentive for an extremely energetic attack on the difficult road to Appleby, with a most unusual 80 at Little Salkeld. The climbing from there to Ais Gill was superb, with no lower speed than 48 on the successive stretches of 1 in 100. Thus Ais Gill box was passed in $22\frac{1}{4}$ minutes from the Appleby start, a clear gain of $1\frac{3}{4}$ minutes despite a 20mph permanent way slack which prevented any rushing of the bank: no less than 1680EDBHP was being produced on this climb.

TABLE 9—UP SHAMROCK, LIVERPOOL LIME ST.—EUSTON

Locomotive: 46164 The Artists' Rifleman
Load: 16 bogies, 528 tons tare 538 tons gross
Driver: Not known

Distance miles		Schedule min	Actual Time min sec	Speed mph
0.0	CREWE	0	0 00	—
4.8	Betley Road		8 20	50
8.0	Madeley		12 09	$51\frac{1}{2}$
10.5	Whitmore	16	15 02	55
14.7	Standon Bridge		18 55	$75\frac{1}{2}$
			eased	
24.5	STAFFORD	30	28 26	*
30.9	Colwich		35 41	64
33.8	RUGELEY	40	38 21	$68\frac{1}{2}$
41.8	LICHFIELD	48	45 34	63
48.1	TAMWORTH	54	50 58	74/68
55.8	Atherstone		58 19	60
61.0	NUNEATON	68	63 23	66/61
64.6	Bulkington		67 24	52
70.0	Brinklow		72 55	66
75.5	RUGBY	84	78 29	*
82.8	Welton		88 38	$54\frac{1}{2}$
88.4	Weedon		94 13	70
95.3	BLISWORTH	106	100 27	65
98.2	Roade	109	103 17	60
103.3	Castlethorpe		107 37	80
105.7	Wolverton		109 30	$76\frac{1}{2}$/66
111.4	BLETCHLEY	123	114 56	—
16.3	Leighton Buzzard		9 20	$63\frac{1}{4}$
10.6	Cheddington		13 23	$59\frac{1}{2}$
15.0	TRING	18	18 06	55
18.7	Berkhamsted		21 40	75
22.2	Hemel Hempstead..		24 37	—
			pws	35
29.2	WATFORD JUNCTION	31	32 37	70
33.4	Hatch End		36 21	65
35.3	Harrow		38 00	74
38.6	Wembley		40 38	79
41.3	WILLESDEN JUNCTION	42	42 53	68
			sig stop	
46.7	EUSTON	51	63 05	—

Net time: 49min

* Permanent speed restriction

[12] Trains Illustrated, October 1959

Nevertheless, it gives me a certain satisfaction to be able to reproduce Table 9 as the ultimate in published power output for a rebuilt Scot, partly because it was on the West Coast main line, which always seemed their natural home, and partly because the engine concerned was the same one as with my footplate trip with Maurice Corbett (Table 5). The train concerned was the up "Shamrock" from Liverpool, and the run dates from 1954[13]. A very large train of 16 coaches, very crowded and grossing 585 tons, was the task, and a 21¾ minute late start from Crewe, the spur.

The climb to Whitmore was an incredible performance, and the firing and the preparation before leaving Crewe must have been superb. No back damper only here, I suspect! For this vast train was lifted up to Betley Road and *then accelerated up the three miles of 1 in 177 to Madeley from 50 to 51½mph*. This required an equivalent DBHP of 1950, and must have involved full regulator working with something like 40 per cent cutoff. This would call for a firing rate of the order of 4500lb/hour, or over 140lb sq ft of grate/hr, far beyond the capacity of one fireman to sustain, and a remarkable testimonial for the double blastpipe and chimney.

And this was no flash in the pan. The acceleration continued on the easier grades, reaching 55 at Whitmore summit, and after the Stafford slack first class work was done on the undulating grades to Rugby with this great train. To pass Tring in 18min 6sec from the Bletchley start, with 585 tons, at 55mph, was further sterling work, calling for some 1510EDBHP. One would look long and far to find finer performance from a 4–6–0 locomotive of 83 tons weight.

On this happy note, let me close. In traffic the Royal Scots are no more. It is good to know that at least one example of this remarkable class has evaded the scrapper's torch and is being restored to its one-time glory. But never again shall we see the big-scale performances I have described, see the sparks carried high in the night sky from those double chimneys, and hear the ring of the fireman's shovel on the firehole as he converts hard Yorkshire coal into horsepower at the driver's command.

[13] *Railway Magazine*, October 1963

Footplate Impressions

by PETER G. JOHNSON

MY FIRST EXPERIENCE of Royal Scot class locomotives was way back in 1950, just after the Railways became nationalised. I was borrowed from the ex-GW shed at Gresty Lane, Crewe, by the then North shed for firing duties on a local passenger from Crewe to Shrewsbury, returning with a West to North express.

On arrival at North shed, my driver, also an ex-Western man, and I were asked by a deputy foreman, "Are you the Western men for the 3.32 Salop?" On replying "Yes," we were informed "6136 on No 2 shed, she's all ready." As a Western man my heart leapt. Blimey! A Scot! A loco I had heard so much about but as yet had no experience on! That was to be rectified as we walked to No 2 shed.

There she stood, No 46136 *The Border Regiment* in all her magnificence. She was "fresh off", in other words a loco fresh from the works after an overhaul, covered in a nice new coat of paint, in this case the new "British Railways" shade of green for express engines.

On boarding the footplate and being a fireman, the first things I inspected were the level of the water in the boiler, the steam pressure gauge and the condition of the fire. As it was fully an hour before we were due off shed, it was not necessary to get a full head of steam. Neither was it necessary to fill the boiler. If the water could be seen in the gauge glass, and, on testing, the water bobbed down and back to its former level, it was satisfactory. Likewise the steam pressure, a Scot was pressed at 250lb/sq in, at which pressure it blew off. As long as there was around 180/200lb it was considered sufficient to test the various fittings: blower valve, both live and exhaust steam injectors, and if in use, the steam heating apparatus.

The fire need not necessarily be "all over the box", in fact it was far better if it wasn't, as in this state the front fire bars could be examined, as could the brick arch and the tubeplate. Examination of the tubeplate is very important, as if a tubeplate was found to be leaking at the corners, or the tubes were caked over or blocked, it would seriously affect the steaming qualities of the loco. It was also very important to examine the fusible lead plugs, of which there were two. One was situated at the front of the firebox crown, and the other at the rear. Should there be the slightest trace of dampness

48

Rebuilding under Stanier—still in wartime black livery No 6117 *Welsh Guardsman* heads a Leeds-Glasgow express out of Carlisle

[*Eric Treacy*

E

In 1943, 6103 *Royal Scots Fusilier* was the first to emerge from Crewe works extensively rebuilt with new taper boiler, double blastpipe and chimney and re-designed cylinders and valves

[BR

View of a rebuilt "Scot" from the footplate

[Eric Treacy

In wartime black No 46146 *The Rifle Brigade* poses outside Holyhead shed
[Eric Treacy

No 46146 *The Rifle Brigade* climbing the bank out of Holyhead station with
the up "Irish Mail"
[Eric Treacy

Left: No 46138 *The London Irish Rifleman* in Lime Street Cutting, Liverpool with up "Merseyside Express".
[Eric Treacy

Facing page: Leaving King's Cross during the 1948 Locomotive Exchange trials is No 46162 *Queen's Westminster Rifleman*
[F. R. Hebron

During the 1948 Exchanges No 46162 *Queen's West-minster Rifleman* leaves Reading with the down 1.30pm Paddington-Plymouth
[M. W. Earley

To provide extra water capacity for its 1948 trials on the trough-less Southern, No 46154 *The Hussar* was paired with a WD 2-8-0 tender. It was photographed near Hook on the down "Atlantic Coast Express"

The 4pm Euston-Manchester Express at Bushey in early
BR days behind No 46121 *Highland Light Infantry, City
of Glasgow Regiment*   [E. R. Wethersett

A Manchester to Euston express shortly after leaving
Rugby in April, 1959 hauled by No 46115 *Scots Guardsman*

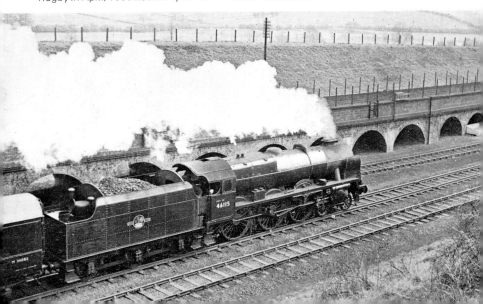

Right: The final version — rebuilt with smoke deflectors: No 46118 *Royal Welsh Fusilier* tops Shap Summit with 1.10pm Euston-Glasgow in August, 1963
[Peter J. Robinson]

Facing page: Even with smoke deflectors the rebuilt "Scots" had a drifting exhaust problem, clearly shown in this view of No 46108 *Seaforth Highlander* heading the down "Thames-Clyde Express" near Sanquhar in July, 1957
[W. J. V. Anderson]

Rebuilt "Scot" and rebuilt "Patriot"—Nos 46123 *Royal Irish Fusilier* and 45521 *Rhyl* ready to leave Leeds City on the 9.55am Newcastle-Liverpool in November 1960
[G. W. Morrison]

A unique experiment with square-shaped deflectors in BR days—No 46106 *Gordon Highlander* on the Sunday 2.30pm Manchester-Birmingham train at Heaton Moor in June, 1954
[T. Lewis]

Close-up of No 46148's nameplate

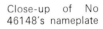

Nameplate of No 6141 *[L. Hanson*

Close up of No 6103's nameplate *[L. Hanson*

Nameplate of No 6118. The polished raised brass letters, beading and regimental badge were set against a black painted ground

[L. Hanson

The first nameplates of No 6121 simply said HLI. The more elaborate version shown here was a later substitution

Above: No 46126 takes water on Whitmore troughs with an up express for Euston on June 16, 1962 *[R. J. Farrell*

Above right: Displaced to the Midland by dieselisation on the West Coast main line—leaving St Pancras with the 1.55pm Manchester express is No 46151 *The Royal Horse Guardsman* in August, 1960

Below right: Final home for No 46163 *Civil Service Rifleman*—the Great Central; it leaves Nottingham with the 11.15am parcels for Marylebone in June, 1963

[Colin P. Walker

Above: Downgraded to freight haulage—No 46139 heads coal empties near Watford
[BR

Centre Right: "Royal Scot" at Oxford—No 46122 *Royal Ulster Rifleman* works a freight from Cowley to Merseyside in May, 1962

Below: No 46152 *The Royal Dragoon*, cab painted with a diagonal stripe to indicate ability to work under 25KV overhead conductor wires, heads the 3.40pm Bradford-Carlisle out of Settle in April, 1965
[P. F. Claxton

Above: "Royal Scot" at Doncaster—No 46162 *Queen's Westminster Rifleman* appears double-heading class A1 4-6-2 No 60128 on a six-coach train from York in August, 1961   *[David C Smith*

Below: "Royal Scot" at Southampton Ocean Terminal, with the *Queen Elizabeth.* No 46141 *The North Staffordshire Regiment* after arrival with a special in February, 1963   *[G. Wheeler*

No 6100 *Royal Scot* at the end of its last journey to serve as a static display at Butlin's Holiday Camp, Skegness, being given a welcome by the band of the 1st Battalion Royal Scots Guards and a "redcoat" guard of honour

[Butlins

Another preserved "Scot"—Lt J. A. Napier, Scots Guards, salutes No 6115 *Scots Guardsman,* which he has just renamed at the Dinting Railway Centre, Glossop, in October, 1969

[David Birch

around the lead centre, the matter should have been reported to the shed foreman fitter immediately, as, if it melted completely letting all the water out of the boiler, great damage would be done to the engine's boiler and firebox. It was also considered a disgrace to "drop one's plugs".

While the fireman was doing his duties as regards engine preparation, the driver was also busy. His job consisted mainly of oiling and examining the locomotive in general. Each moving part or knuckle joint had an oiling point, accessible by removing the cork from its position to reveal the oiling point. The cavity was filled with oil and the cork firmly replaced. On rare occasions I have known one oiling point to take more than $1\frac{1}{2}$ pints of oil—the amount used depended upon how far the engine had come since it was last oiled.

On the Royal Scot class there was not only the outside motion to oil, but, as they were 3-cylinder locomotives, there was a motion underneath; at Crewe it was customary for the fireman to oil this, and what a job it was! If the engine was set right, with the inside big end at the bottom, the fireman could climb up in front of the big end balance web and sit precariously on the inside connecting rod, and, without getting down again, he could oil all the necessary parts. Unless of course he was unlucky enough to drop one of the seven corks or run short of oil. If this happened, he had to clamber down, only to climb up again, and continue. There were also the bogie oil keeps to top up, though these were comparatively easy to get at, being situated on the inside of the axle hub.

On my first trip with 46136, all this was done for me by the preparing fireman. My experiences, trials and tribulations regarding preparation came much later.

At the appointed time, after levelling the fire all over the firebox, and filling the tank to capacity we arrived at the exit signal with 46136. After reporting off shed and getting the exit "dummy" off, away we went, slowly, over the maze of pointwork at Crewe North Junction.

As I sat on my seat and looked ahead, I compared my strange steed with the engines of similar build I was used to, namely the GW Granges, Halls and the occasional Star. Of course, the great difference was that I was on the "wrong" side, all Western engines being right-hand drive, whereas the Scot was left-hand drive. It took me quite a while to get used to sitting and working on the right-hand side and I never did master firing from my own side, and often used to stick my backside on the driver's lap. I also seemed to be much higher up, both the track and smokebox seemed so far away and the

F

cab felt so wide. I think this was due to the cab extending to the outer sides of the mainframes, unlike a Western locomotive upon which one could gain the framing from the cab as there was a foothold the whole length of the cab, On a Scot, however, the cab was flush and the framing could only be gained from the steps by the front buffer beam. These then were my first impressions of a Scot from the footplate.

Eventually, after negotiating Crewe Station we backed on to our train, a mere three coaches, the weight of the loco being very nearly as much as the tonnage of the train. Alongside us in No 3 bay (we stood in No 4 bay) stood the 3.15pm ex-GW train, all stations to Wellington. At its head was the usual 51XX Prairie tank. I remember looking at it and thinking how small it looked from my Scot.

At precisely 3.32pm we were away, and as my driver opened the regulator I was to hear for the first time (but by no means the last) the characteristic sound of a Scot's beat—a sort of "Chi-Chi-Chi-Cha-Cha-Cha, Chi-Chi-Chi-Cha-Cha-Cha". Of course there were variations in the sound, for instance when the loco slipped violently on starting with a heavy train, and when a Scot was really opened up and put at a bank. This developed into a full-throated roar, and if the fireman was not quite ready, his fire would be torn to pieces by the engine blast.

There was none of this on my first trip, however. We ambled merrily along through the green fields of Cheshire and the rolling Shropshire plains, stopping at all stations. I was, if anything, making a far harder task of firing than was required. I remember arriving at Shrewsbury with the firebox full and the boiler full, and got myself and the driver greatly disliked, as the safety valves unfortunately blew off in the station, which was a nuisance to everybody.

Our load on the return was much heavier—twelve coaches—and we were non-stop to Crewe. We were now determined to see what our Scot would do.

After slight slipping, we made a put at Hadnall Bank and we were amazed at the ease with which *The Border Regiment* went up it. With no more than half regulator and 20 per cent cut-off we sailed along. Whitchurch was reached in no time, and I decided I had better work my fire down so as not to arrive on Crewe North with a lot of fire in the box. On looking in the firebox I saw to my amazement that it was full very nearly to the arch. It would be impossible to burn all this lot to Crewe, so my driver increased cut-off to about 35 per cent and then I heard the roar from the chimney end and saw great lumps of red-hot coal being send skywards. I expected the steam pressure to fall drastically but it didn't, it actually started to rise even though the exhaust injector was on.

All too soon we arrived at Crewe, the fire now white hot and the valves just below blowing off. Needless to say the firebox was still too full. We detached ourselves from the train and returned to the North Shed. A driver and fireman who had been sent to relieve us shook their heads sadly when they saw the state of the boiler and the firebox.

This first trip on a Scot whetted my appetite for more, and I resolved that I would transfer as soon as possible from the Western to the North Shed in my grade as fireman.

Before this came about, I was once again borrowed from Gresty Lane to go as passenger to Holyhead to work a return train, my driver this time being a regular North Shed man. The loco on this occasion was once again a Scot, No 46142 *The York and Lancaster Regiment* and the train worked this time was the 1.10 "Irish Mail". The load to me was a colossal one of seventeen coaches. I need not have worried with this driver, used to such loads, who knew exactly what a Scot could do. The trip was uneventful, except that under the guiding hand of the driver I found I only burned half the amount of coal I should have, had I had my own way. I was now eager more than ever to become a North Shed fireman.

My dream came true in 1952 when the powers that be at last allowed a fireman a move in the grade. I applied for the transfer and got my position in the North Shed in September 1952, my seniority placing me in No 6 link, the Birmingham link—more affectionately known as the "Brumijem" link. In this link Scots predominated. Both early and late Glasgow–Birmingham trains were rostered in No 6 link, and on these trains there were, more often than not, the last remaining unrebuilt Scots. No 46110 *Grenadier Guardsman*, No 46134 *The Cheshire Regiment*, No 46137 *The Prince of Wales Volunteers* (*South Lancashire*), No 46148 *The Manchester Regiment*, No 46151 *The Royal Horse Guardsman* and No 46163 *Civil Service Rifleman* being regular performers.

Far more skill was required at both driving and firing the unre-built locomotives. Normally they would not take a thick fire and they needed the "little and often" technique (much to the Crewe North firing inspector's pleasure). In my early days as a fireman at Crewe North, I have often been down for steam on an unrebuilt Scot owing to firing the engine too heavily. The exhaust steam in-jector was very different on one of these—it was what was termed "double-barrelled". This had a separate steam valve wheel for the exhaust steam. The idea was that when the water feed was opened, and when the locomotive was working with regulator open, the exhaust steam wheel was opened and the injector should work. With the regulator closed the live steam wheel was opened to assist the exhaust steam to work the injector. The principle was very similar to the exhaust injector on a GW engine.

After promotion to No 5 link, I had my first taste of what a rebuilt Scot was really capable of. One of the jobs rostered in this link was up to London with the morning "Ulster Express", and after taking rest at the Railway Hostel at Camden, returning with the 12.2am Euston to Crewe, diagrammed to a Scot each way. The up train would be remanned at Crewe, the engine coming from Morecambe. Very often the coal was way back in the tender upon arrival at Crewe, and after a brief pause for platform duties you were "right away" Euston. The load was usually a very heavy one, possibly 14 or 15 coaches, on rare occasions maybe more. My driver in this link used to say, "The hardest job was to clear Stafford in 29 minutes", though personally I found the hardest job was between Bletchley and Tring. By this time all the coal had to be handled twice as it was well back in the tender. You had to either shovel it to the front of the tender or pull it down with the coal pick, and then bang it in the box. Then you had to get more coal down, by which time the box needed attention again so in went that lot, and then up the tender again and so on until the long downhill gradient of Tring was reached. You enjoyed a sit-down and a smoke by then. Two of the most regular performers on this job were Nos 46167 *The Hertfordshire Regiment* and 46154 *The Hussars*.

The return job was the 12.2am and after a day in bed at Camden one was ready for the fray again. First of all the loco had to be prepared at Camden Shed and then backed down on to the train at Euston. This too was a heavy train, at least half the vehicles being parcels vans. The 12.2 was not a very fast train—more of an endurance test really—as it stopped at all principal stations to Crewe via Birmingham, not arriving at Crewe until 5.30am, where once again the tender would be looking rather bare. The continual stopping for long periods and then getting going again played havoc with the fire and it was always in a very clinkered state on arival at Crewe.

On being transferred to the Glasgow link, I had my first experience of the formidable banks of Shap and Beattock with a Scot. Provided the fire was in a reasonable condition no trouble would be experienced with steaming. Several miles before the actual climb began the fireman would start building up the fire gradually, so that when it became necessary for the loco to be opened up the fire was in a state to take the hammering to which it was subjected.

In this link, one of the jobs from Glasgow was the 11.15 Glasgow–Birmingham as far as Crewe, stopping at Motherwell, Carstairs and Carlisle. This was always rostered to a Polmadie (66A) Scot, regular performers being No 46102 *Black Watch*, No 46104 *Scottish Borderer*, No 46105 *Cameron Highlander*, No 46107 *Argyll and Sutherland Highlander* and No 46121 *Highland Light Infantry, City of Glasgow Regiment*. Out of all these 46104 was the worst engine I ever worked on. I fired this locomotive countless times and never did make it steam correctly; somewhere there was a secret of how to fire it, but I never found it. The Polmadie Scots were notorious rough riders and 46104 was no exception. I have arrived at Crewe "black and blue", battered because of the roughness of this particular engine. Whereas other Scots would swing left round a particular curve, 46104 would sway the opposite way throwing one completely off balance, and if one happened to have a shovelful of coal on the swing at the time the driver received most of it on his feet!

It was in this link that I remanned a Scot from Euston for Glasgow. Because of a last-minute failure, No 46117 *Welsh Guardsman*, one of the converted Leeds (Holbeck) engines was provided to work the train. She steamed and rode like a coach all the way and she was far from being a "fresh off". Leeds seemed to look after their engines and it was very rare for them to be off their beaten track. 46117 was this time, though I never did find out why.

As I passed through the links at Crewe North, I had many trips on Royal Scots both good types and bad, over short and long distances, with heavy loads and light ones. I fired to drivers who hardly pushed the smoke from the chimney so expansively did they set the cut-off. At the other end of the scale, I had drivers who believed in keeping the chimney end free of smoke, also the fireman very busy, for twice as much coal was heaved into the box!

By the time I was passed out as a driver, the Scots were still going but they were slowly getting relegated to second class work by an influx of diesels. Somehow, whenever I was called upon for driving duties on the main line. I always seemed to have any class of engine bar a Scot. Why they seemed to elude me I don't know—but they did. On a Scot diagram, I would have "Lizzies", "Baby Scots", 5XP Jubilees and even a Black Five, but never a Scot, until one day I was called upon to work a special excursion to Wembley. The event was a Girls' Hockey International and I was routed all the diverse ways possible from Crewe, picking up en-route.

Once again I experienced my first feeling of pride when I found out that my loco was No 46147 *The Northamptonshire Regiment;* at last I had a "Scot", and after leaving Crewe. I was determined to show my young passengers and their charges what a Scot could do. The load was quite considerable and the station delays, for various reasons, were long and we left Stafford, our last stop, 48 minutes late. (We travelled via Whitchurch, Wellington and Newport from Crewe to Stafford and stopped at all stations!)

After leaving Stafford, I opened out 46147 and attempted to cut some of the arrears using little "hints" of driving technique I had picked up from the many drivers I had fired for. My steed was a good one and the fireman was willing, and in no time at all my speed was up into the seventies. It is sufficient to say time was indeed made up. My first experience of being in charge of a Scot was a very favourable one.

I had several trips with Scots after that and always found them willing even though at that time they were becoming very run down. I shall always remember being in charge of No 46139 *The Welch Regiment* on a Crewe–Carlisle semi-fast, and somewhere north of Penrith (our last stop before Carlisle) I endeavoured to get the magical "ton" out of her. Regrettably I failed, by a mere 3mph.

This is how it happened. On ready to leave Penrith, next stop Carlisle, my fireman informed me that if possible he would like a pint at Carlisle. I replied that I would do my best! The load was a mere six coaches and the road was a gradual downhill glide, all the way to Carlisle.

We got the tip to leave Penrith and away we went, half-open regulator being used and around 50 per cent cut-off until the speed got around the 30/35mph mark. As our speed increased I eased the cut-off back until it was about 25 per cent, still keeping half-open regulator. When the speed had reached the 80s and appeared to be stationary around 83, I increased the regulator opening to two-thirds and gradually got my speed up into the 90s as the road was favourable; speed still increased until it was 95mph.

I knew by my knowledge of the road that if I did not reach the magical "ton" within the next mile or so, I should have to abandon the attempt as there was a permanent speed restriction of 70mph around Wreay curve. We were now approaching Southwaite, in a last attempt to reach 100mph I opened the regulator wide and speed reached 97mph and was still rising, regrettably we shot past Southwaite and I realised I was running out of track as Wreay curve was very close. I reluctantly had to close the regulator and apply the brake. As it was we took the curve at a far higher speed than the restriction permitted us to. Once round the curve it was far too near Carlisle to attempt any more speed so we coasted into Carlisle just in time for my mate to get his pint.

Had I opened 46139 out to full regulator sooner I may have touched the 100mph mark, this I cannot say, it was the only time I attempted the "ton" on this stretch of track, indeed it was the only chance, as I never had a loco decent enough to attempt it again. Of course at this time they were banned from the line south of Crewe owing to electrification clearances.

My most vivid memory of a Scot was way back in 1953. I was still a fireman then, and was standing in the up loop at Hartford, a few miles north of Crewe, with an up freight, awaiting the passage of the up "Red Rose", the 5.25pm Liverpool–Euston. The main line "pegs" were off and I could hear her coming, working hard. As she roared past I saw that it was not the customary class of engine in charge, a Duchess or a Princess, but the very last of the straight-boilered Scots, No 46156 *The South Wales Borderer*. It was being flailed along in typical North Western style by its Edge Hill driver, as the firework display from the chimney bore evidence. I later found out that the regular Duchess had failed at Lime Street at the last minute and 46156 had been commandeered from a local passenger to deputise. This then is my lasting memory of and epitaph to, a famous locomotive class.

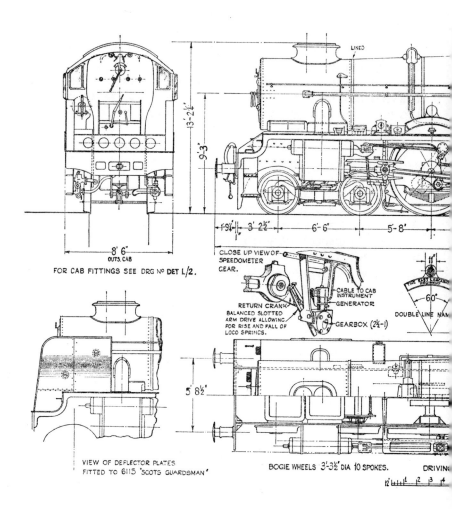

13'-2¼"

9'-3"

8' 6"
OUTS. CAB

FOR CAB FITTINGS SEE DRG Nº DET L/2.

1'-9¼" 3' 2½" 6'- 6" 5'- 8"

LINED

CLOSE UP VIEW OF
SPEEDOMETER
GEAR.

CABLE TO CAB
INSTRUMENT
GENERATOR
RETURN CRANK
BALANCED SLOTTED
ARM DRIVE ALLOWING
FOR RISE AND FALL OF
LOCO SPRINGS. GEARBOX (2½-1)

1¼"
60°
DOUBLE LINE NAM

5' 8½"

VIEW OF DEFLECTOR PLATES
FITTED TO 6115 'SCOTS GUARDSMAN'

BOGIE WHEELS 3'-3½" DIA 10 SPOKES. DRIVING

12"   1   2   3   4

The standard rebuilt Royal Scot locomotive.
The original design is shown on pages 24
and 25

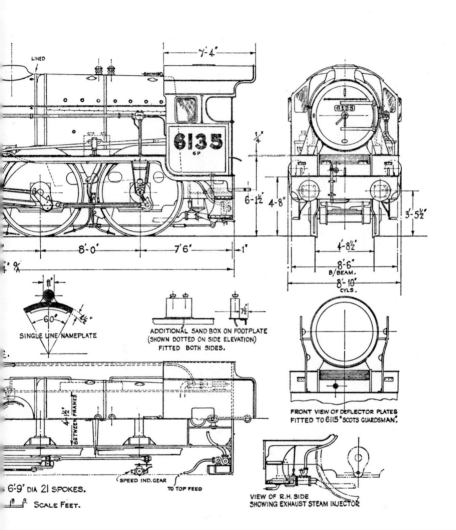

LINED

7'-4"

6135
6P

6-1½" 4-8"

8'-0" 7'6" 1"

4-8½"

3'-5½"

8'-6"
B/BEAM.

8'-10"
CYLS.

60°

SINGLE LINE NAMEPLATE

7½"

ADDITIONAL SAND BOX ON FOOTPLATE
(SHOWN DOTTED ON SIDE ELEVATION)
FITTED BOTH SIDES.

FRONT VIEW OF DEFLECTOR PLATES
FITTED TO 6115 "SCOTS GUARDSMAN".

4-½"
BETWEEN FRAMES

SPEED IND. GEAR

6'-9" DIA 21 SPOKES.

SCALE FEET.

TO TOP FEED

VIEW OF R.H. SIDE
SHOWING EXHAUST STEAM INJECTOR

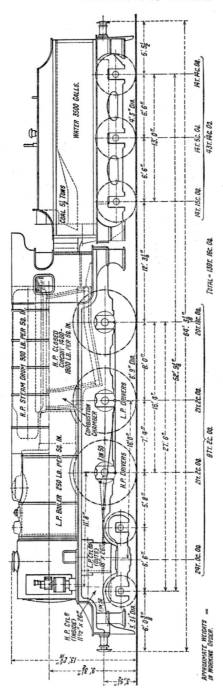

Drawing for the original high pressure locomotive No 6399 *Fury*. After the boiler blew up it was reconstructed to the design shown below

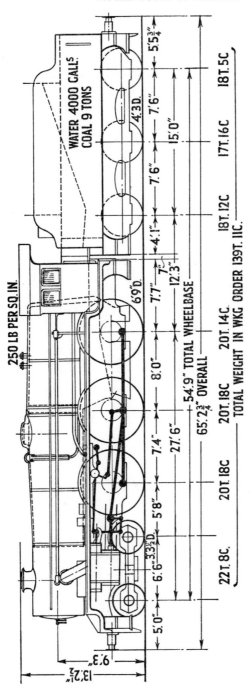

No 6170 *British Legion*—the Stanier rebuild of the experimental locomotive *Fury*. It was basically the prototype for the later rebuilding of the entire Royal Scot class although the rest of the class had the standard G2 boiler and not the unique G2A boiler on 6170

Appendices

Dimensions

	ROYAL SCOT	CONVERTED SCOT
Cylinders (3)..	18in 26in	18in 26in
Driving wheel diameter	6ft 9in	6ft 9in
Grate Area (sq ft)	31.2	31.25
Heating Surface (sq ft)		
Firebox	189	195
Tubes	1,892	1,667
Superheater	399	357
Total	2,480	2,219
Flue gas area (sq ft)	5.2	5.0
Boiler pressure (lb/sq in)	250	250
Nominal tractive effort (lb)	33,000	33,000
Valve diameter (in)	9	9
Valve Lap (in)	1.5	1.5
Valve Lead (in)	0.25	0.25
Adhesion weight (ton)	62½	61
Total weight (ton)	85	83

Performances

Engine Class	Original	Original	Converted	Converted	Converted
Engine No	6125	6131	46162		46104
Load (ton)	375	470	480	515	550
Miles	77.2	152.7	16.8	77.2	23.8
Minutes	62.8	142	16.07	65.3	29.6
Mean speed, mph	73.7	64.5	62.6	71.0	48.2
Estimated DHP	1060	1120	1400	1350	1220
DHP/Grate Area	34	36	45	43	39
Percentage of Standard*	90	105	105	115	97
Route	Rugby—Willesden	Crewe—Willesden	Lavington—Savernake	Rugby—Willesden	†Carstairs—Beattock Summit

†Start; at all other places the train was timed as it passed

*A "high-class standard" representative of the best efforts of pre-nationalisation locomotive classes

Names and Important Dates

LMS No	Name	Original name until 1935/6	Date rebuilt	Date re-numbered	With-drawn
6100	*Royal Scot		6/50	6/48	10/62 (1)
6101	Royal Scots Grey		11/45	5/48	9/63
6102	*Black Watch		10/49	9/48	12/62
6103	Royal Scots Fusilier		6/43	10/48	12/62 (2)
6104	Scottish Borderer		3/46	8/48	12/62
6105	*Cameron Highlander		3/48	5/48	12/62
6106	*Gordon Highlander		9/49	6/48	12/62
6107	*Argyll and Sutherland Highlander		2/50	4/48	12/62
6108	Seaforth Highlander		8/43	5/48	1/63
6109	Royal Engineer		7/43	5/48	12/62
6110	*Grenadier Guardsman		1/53	3/49	2/64
6111	Royal Fusilier		10/47	11/48	10/63
6112	Sherwood Forester		9/43	9/48	5/64
6113	*Cameronian		12/50	5/49	12/62
6114	Coldstream Guardsman		6/46	6/48	10/63
6115	Scots Guardsman		8/47	1/49	1/66 (3)
6116	Irish Guardsman		8/44	9/48	9/63
6117	Welsh Guardsman		12/43	5/48	11/62
6118	Royal Welch Fusilier		12/46	2/49	6/64
6119	Lancashire Fusilier		9/44	7/48	12/63
6120	Royal Inniskilling Fusilier		11/44	6/48	7/63
6121	Highland Light Infantry, City of Glasgow Regiment (in LMS period, plain H.L.I.)		8/46	10/48	12/62
6122	Royal Ulster Rifleman		9/45	4/48	11/64
6123	*Royal Irish Fusilier		5/49	6/48	10/62
6124	London Scottish		12/43	4/48	12/62
6125	3rd Carabinier	Lancashire Witch	8/43	9/48	10/64
6126	Royal Army Service Corps	Sanspareil	6/45	11/48	10/63
6127	Old Contemptibles	Novelty	8/44	5/48	12/62
6128	The Lovat Scouts	Meteor	6/46	2/49	5/65
6129	The Scottish Horse	Comet	12/44	6/48	6/64
6130	*The West Yorkshire Regiment	Liverpool	12/49	5/48	12/62
6131	The Royal Warwickshire Regiment	Planet	10/44	8/48	10/62
6132	The Kings Regiment, Liverpool	Phoenix	11/43	4/48	2/64
6133	The Green Howards	Vulcan	7/44	1/49	2/63
6134	*The Cheshire Regiment	Atlas	12/54	11/48	11/62
6135	The East Lancashire Regiment	Samson	1/47	9/48	12/62
6136	*The Border Regiment	Goliath	3/50	7/48	4/64
6137	*The Prince of Wales' Volunteers (South Lancashire)	Vesta	3/55	5/48	10/62 (4)
6138	The London Irish Rifleman	Fury (until 1929)	6/44	1/48	2/63
6139	The Welch Regiment	Ajax	11/46	5/48	10/62
6140	*The Kings Royal Rifle Corps	Hector	5/52	1/49	11/65
6141	*The North Staffordshire Regiment	Caledonian	10/50	7/48	4/64

LMS No	Name	Original name until 1935/6	Date rebuilt	Date re-numbered	With-drawn
6142	*The York and Lancaster Regiment	Lion	2/51	7/48	1/64
6143	*The South Staffordshire Regiment	Mail	6/49	9/48	12/63
6144	Honourable Artillery Company	Ostrich	6/45	6/48	1/64
6145	The Duke of Wellington's Regt. (West Riding)	Condor	1/44	9/49	11/62
6146	The Rifle Brigade	Jenny Lind	10/43	6/48	11/62
6147	The Northamptonshire Regiment	Courier	9/46	1/49	11/62
6148	*The Manchester Regiment	Velocipede	7/54	6/48	12/64
6149	The Middlesex Regiment	Lady of the Lake	4/45	4/48	9/63
6150	The Life Guardsman		12/45	1/49	12/62
6151	*The Royal Horse Guardsman		4/53	10/48	12/62
6152	The King's Dragoon Guardsman		8/45	6/48	4/65 (5)
6153	*The Royal Dragoon		8/49	6/48	12/62
6154	*The Hussar		3/48	4/48	11/62 (6)
6155	*The Lancer		8/50	7/48	12/64
6156	*The South Wales Borderer		5/54	1/49	10/64
6157	The Royal Artilleryman		1/46	12/48	1/64
6158	*The Loyal Regiment		9/52	10/48	11/63
6159	The Royal Air Force		10/45	9/48	11/62
6160	Queen Victoria's Rifleman		2/45	9/48	5/65
6161	King's Own		10/46	7/48	11/62
6162	*Queen's Westminster Rifleman		1/48	4/48	6/64
6163	*Civil Service Rifleman		10/53	11/48	9/64
6164	*The Artists' Rifleman		6/51	4/48	12/62
6165	*The Ranger (12th London Regt.)		6/52	10/48	12/64
6166	London Rifle Brigade		1/45	7/48	10/64
6167	*The Hertfordshire Regiment		12/48	12/48	4/64
6168	The Girl Guide		4/46	9/48	5/64
6169	The Boy Scout		5/45	5/48	7/63
6170	British Legion	Fury (as 6399)	1935	4/48	11/62

* Still with parallel boiler at close of LMS period
(1) Original 6152 until 1933. Preserved as LMS 6100 by Sir Billy Butlin but still in re-built condition. The first of the class to be withdrawn
(2) The first genuine rebuilt engine
(3) Last engine to be withdrawn (actually on 1/1/66) and believed first to get smoke deflectors in rebuilt state (8/47)
(4) Last engine to be rebuilt
(5) Original 6100 until 1933
(6) Actually withdrawn for rebuilding in 1947

Building dates:
6101-49/6152 built 1927 by NB Locomotive Co.
6100/6150-1/6153-69 built 1929 at Derby Works.
6399 built 1929 by NB Locomotive Co.
6170 and all other rebuilds were completed at Crewe works.
Engines fitted with experimental smoke deflection apparatus prior to adoption of large side-shields: 6100, 6125, 6133, 6161.

Acknowledgements to David Jenkinson, article 'The Royal Scots', *Railway World*, October, 1967.